MISTER GOOD MORNING

Mister Good Morning

stories of flesh, blood and holy spirit

Murray Andrew Pura

REGENT COLLEGE PUBLISHING
VANCOUVER, CANADA

Mister Good Morning
Copyright ©1999 by Murray Andrew Pura

First printing by Regent College Publishing, an imprint of the
Regent College Bookstore,
5800 University Boulevard, Vancouver, B.C. Canada V6T 2E4

E-mail: bookstore@regent-college.edu
Website: www.regent-bookstore.com
Orders toll-free: 1-800-334-3279

The views expressed in works published by
Regent College Publishing
are those of the author and may not necessarily
represent the official position of Regent College.

Printed in the United States of America

Canadian Cataloguing in Publication Data

Pura, Murray, 1954-
Mister Goodmorning

ISBN 0-88865-424-3 (Canada)
ISBN 1-57383-134-4 (U.S.)

I. Title.
PS8581.U65M57 1999   C813'.54   C99-910147-1
PR9199.3.P778M57 1999

For Rose, my mother
and Paul, my father

the boy born on Bobby Burns day
became a writer

Contents

Preface

Stories hold a prominent role in revealing God and God's ways to us. Storytellers in our Christian communities carry a major responsibility for keeping us alert to these stories and the way stories work. Our best storytellers learn their craft from Jesus, famous for using the story to involve his listeners in recognizing and dealing with God in their lives.

In both the Old and the New Testaments of our Christian scriptures story is the primary verbal means of bringing God's word to us. For that we can be most grateful, for story is our most accessible form of speech. Young and old love stories. Literate and illiterate alike tell and listen to stories. Neither stupidity nor sophistication put us outside the magnetic field of story. The only serious rival to story in terms of accessibility and attraction is song, and there are plenty of those in the Bible too.

But there is another reason for the appropriateness of story as a major means of bringing us God's word. Story doesn't just tell us something and leave it there, it invites our participation. A good storyteller gathers us into the story. We feel emotions, get caught up in the drama, identify with the characters, see into nooks and crannies of life that we had overlooked, realize there is more to this business of being human than we had yet explored. If the storyteller is good, doors and windows open. Murray Pura is one of the good ones, good in both the artistic and moral senses.

Honest stories respect our freedom; they don't manipulate us, don't force us, don't distract us from life. They show us a spacious world in which God creates and saves and blesses. First through our imaginations and then through our faith—imagination and faith are close kin here—they offer us a place in the story, invite us into this large story that takes place under the broad skies of God's purposes in contrast to the gossipy anecdotes that we cook up in the stuffy closet of the self.

Not all stories, of course, are honest. There are sentimentalizing stories that seduce us into escaping from life; there are propagandistic stories that attempt to enlist us in a cause or bully us into stereotyped response.

And so when an honest storyteller comes along, a storyteller who is at home in the Christian revelation and also respects our dignity and freedom, we are grateful. Murray Pura's stories don't present us with a moral code and tell us, "Live up to this"; nor do they fashion a system of doctrine and say, "Think like this and you will have eternal life." They *invite* us in as participants in something larger than our sin-defined needs, into something truer than our culture-stunted ambitions. We read these stories and recognize ourselves as participants, whether willing or unwilling, in the life of God.

But somehow in our times, story has been pushed from its biblical front-line prominence to a bench on the sidelines, condescended to as "illustration" or "testimony" or "inspirational."

Our contemporary unbiblical preference, both inside and outside the church, is for information over story. We typically gather impersonal (pretentiously called "scientific" or "theological") information, whether doctrinal or philosophical or historical, in order to take things into our own hands and take charge of how we will live our lives. And we commonly consult outside experts to interpret the information for us. But we don't live our lives by information; we live them in relationships in the context of a community of men and women, each one an intricate bundle of experience and motive and desire, and of a personal God who has designs on us for justice and salvation. Information-gathering and consultation of experts leaves out nearly everything that is uniquely *us*—our personal histories and relationships, our sins and guilt, our moral character and believing obedience to God. Telling a story is the primary verbal way of accounting for life the way we live it in actual day-by-day reality. There are no (or few) abstractions in a story—story is immediate, concrete, plotted, relational, personal. And so when we lose touch with our lives, our *souls*—our moral and spiritual, God-personal lives—story is the best verbal way of getting us back in touch again. Which is why God's Word is given for the most part in the form of story.

Welcome to this fresh world of story in which Murray Pura opens our eyes to see, not God in our stories, but our stories in God's story.

Eugene H. Peterson
Professor Emeritus of Spiritual Theology
Regent College, Vancouver, B.C.

1

The Divine Game of Pinzatski

A curious and entertaining game was played by Ellen Pinzatski and her husband. They only played it once a year and then only when they were camped out far in the mountains by a silent turquoise lake they had named Infrequent. The game consisted of one of them pointing out a natural object, a moss-swaddled cedar stump or a high and voluminous cloud formation, and the other stating, to the best of their ability, what characteristic of God was expressed in that object. The idea for the game had arisen from Paul's statement in Romans: "Since the creation of the world God's invisible qualities—his eternal power and divine nature—have been clearly seen, being understood from what has been made." No sort of score was kept, and there were no rules, except that the person interpreting the natural object had to be able to explain to the other, if it was not patently obvious, how they had come to see a particular aspect of God's being manifested in the stump or cloud or grazing elk. The game would go on for hours, days, weeks, as long as the two of them were able to stay in their tent by the lakeside. Once they had retired—both worked and they had no children—there was, of course, much more time for the game. They never tired of it.

I first heard about the game when I was chatting with Arthur, Ellen's husband, after a church study group on the nature of God. Arthur explained how Ellen and he played the game by Lake Infrequent every year, toyed with his teacup as we discussed God's various characteristics, and finally asserted, "Abstractions are a poor second cousin to analogies. Analogies always get you closer to the truth. Never rely on an abstraction if you can get an analogy."

This coming from a professor of mathematics and physics! I asked him why he felt this was so. "Because abstractions establish distance," he answered, "cool, logical, objective distance. Analogies get you in close so you can smell the sweat. They're warm-blooded, make you feel something. That's why the Bible is loaded with them when it gets down to talking about God."

I mentioned the theory that the Bible was loaded with analogies because it was addressed primarily to an uneducated and naive peasant population. Arthur snorted. "If you believe that," he told me, "you'll believe anything."

Perhaps it was this exchange that led to the Pinzatski's invitation to join them on a camping trip that August. I was purportedly an Old Testament scholar, at least Princeton had said so, and they may have felt I needed a good dose of the analogical to set my lecture notes straight. I took them up on the invitation, if for no other reason than to get out of the city for a week. I threw a few pairs of jeans into a dufflebag, a bottle of insect repellent, and a canteen. They had been quite firm about doing all the cooking. "Think of it as spending a week at our house," said Ellen. "Would you bring over your own plate and fork?"

❉

The drive to Lake Infrequent was long, about nine or ten hours. Part of the highway ran through pale desert, but the lake itself was situated among a rush of trees, high above on a plateau, a good hour down a potholed track that shook my teeth. The four-person tent was erected. Ellen got a fire going and Arthur started wrapping corn cobs in aluminum foil. I had just brought several containers of water up from the lake when Ellen said in a clear voice: "Ash."

Arthur looked up from his cornhusking. "Ash," he repeated. "I can't believe we've never talked about that one before."

I set the water down. The pair of them were oblivious to me. Arthur took his time, rolled a few more cobs of corn into tight foil bundles.

2

Finally, he responded: "The purity of God."

"How so?" demanded Ellen, raking white coals to another area of the fire so they could be used for cooking purposes.

"Because God uses fire to purify what is unholy, reducing it to ash."

"But God also uses fire to burn what is holy and reduce it to ash," retorted Ellen. "Think of a holy sacrifice."

"All right," mumbled Arthur, bringing a bowl of wrapped corn cobs over to the fire and placing them on the coals. "But whatever God uses the fire for, ash symbolizes something that has been consumed because the purity of God required it."

While they were eating the meal, Arthur pointed to the ground in front of him as he was chewing. "What would you say about that, Ellen?" Ten or twelve ants were staggering off under bits of corn that had fallen in the dirt.

Ellen laughed. "I think we've come close to something like this before, but okay, I'll go with it. To me, these ants express God's desire to use what is apparently weak and puny to do those tasks which are most difficult and arduous. God is rarely the show-off. Most of the time he likes to work at the big things quietly, operating from a person we'd least expect his power to be present in. I think it is also to do with God's innate pleasure in surprises. It may also have something to do with his sense of humour."

"Good," commented Arthur, sipping at his tin mug of coffee. "Good."

When we were rinsing the plates down by the lake and the sun set in a line of bright green, Ellen asked, "And this particular sunset?"

"This particular sunset," responded Arthur, using a bit of sand to clean grease off his plate, "I would say it expresses the peacefulness of God, that inner tranquility represented by his use of the colour green in the creation of pastures and meadows and forests. In fact, green is the dominant colour found both on dry land and under the sea, indicating God's preference for it and suggesting that a great deal of his character is bound into a correct understanding of that colour and all its shades."

I could not believe the Pinzatskis took the game so seriously and I told Arthur this as the two of us were putting out the fire. Sparks glittered at our feet like a distant galaxy. Arthur poked a large orange coal with his stick. "Who is to say," he asked me, "which is the proper way of approaching God and the universe? As a child or with a pretense to sophistication?"

The game got underway again the next morning after breakfast while we were hiking along the lakeshore. Arthur mentioned the trout basking in the sunlit shadows. Ellen said it had to do with God's pleasure in creating freshwater creatures who enjoyed a lazy moment as much as any human did. In the afternoon, when we reached an alpine meadow that was solid yellow with flowers, Arthur said it had to do with God's extravagance, what he called, "The appropriate slaughter of the fatted calf at the appointed season." On another meadow that was windswept and barren of colour, when Arthur's hand inadvertently revealed a tiny, hidden flower of a purple tint, Ellen declared it had to do with God's frugality. I laughed.

"So a balance is struck," I said.

"Of course," Arthur responded soberly. "God is all balances struck."

By the third day, I was ready for the city. It was not that the game was the only thing that was being verbalized. Far from it. Arthur discussed his work in the field of physics quite freely and Ellen was not adverse to debating the finer points of Shakespeare or James Joyce. But I began to feel I was seeing the world as they did and this was a disturbing sensation. Ellen would point out something and I would come up with an answer faster than Arthur, though I never vocalized it, and I knew I was really in trouble when I began to mull over whether my interpretation of the natural object was closer to the truth about God than Arthur's or Ellen's.

On the fourth day, I was considering various excuses or ploys I might use in order to get them to return to the city a few days early. I could always tell them I needed to revise some of my lecture notes because of our camping trip and that I needed to do this before classes began the following Tuesday. We were hiking high on a ridge of boulders and dead grey trees and I had decided to spring this excuse on them the moment we stopped for lunch when an immense shadow passed over my face and an incredibly violent beating of wings filled my head. I thought of death, ducked my head, threw myself down on the ground.

"My God!" cried Ellen.

I lifted my head and a large bird was there, dark and light and fiercely beaked, moving like a scythe across the sun's arc. Arthur was the first to react.

"Ellen!" he called out. "Golden eagle!"

It was obvious that they had never come across a golden eagle in the wild before. Ellen, gaping after the bird, did not respond. I got to my knees and watched the enormous eagle drop towards a white mountain.

"Freedom," I said. "God's freedom to be God without a single chain, a single restraint. His utter liberty to be the wild God."

The three of us stared after the eagle until it was too small. Then we looked at one another, smiled and continued our hike. I said nothing about going back to the city at lunch. A line had been crossed. I would now play the game along with Ellen and Arthur.

The next three days were a brilliant collage. Nothing was inanimate anymore, but neither did anything exist in terms of its own spirit as an animist would have it. Every rock and tree and bird became a flicker of God's fingers, a certain tilt of his head, a play of light and darkness in his eyes. Doors to God were springing open throughout the entire cosmos and I gazed as a child gazes at his first thunderstorm. I peered at God through flames, through water, glimpsed him in the visage of a doe. His laughter rang out of the throats of birds, his shout was in the waterfall, I heard him whistling to himself as a wind scoured the cliffs and deadfall. At night, I did not sleep under stars but under God.

＊

This was not the only camping trip I took with Ellen and Arthur. Over the next six years I joined them each August for a week by Lake Infrequent. I actually did revise my lecture notes, not once, but four or five times. And our three imaginations became virtually inseparable.

The final night we ever camped together Arthur and I put out the fire once more. Sparks whirled as Arthur stirred with his stick.

"Man is born to trouble," he quoted from Job, "as the sparks fly upwards."

"Meaning what about God?" I challenged him.

He did not hesitate. "Meaning God is not soft. If he thinks a person needs to go through something in order to carve more glory out of him or her, he'll do it. He might weep, but he'll do it."

Four months later, Arthur was diagnosed with cancer of the lung, the liver, and the stomach. They opened him, took a look, and stitched him back up again. They gave him maybe half a year. When I saw him at church after the diagnosis, he had lost weight but not his wit. He pointed at his chest and asked me, "What does this say about God?"

I shook my head, kept my lips in a straight line.

Arthur laughed. "The resurrection of the body. God is not interested in phantoms. That's why the earth is an earth of substance. The Incarnation, my friend, the Incarnation. He's committed himself."

Arthur was not the kind to take a lot of drugs or to end his days between four white walls. "When this cancer releases me," he said, "it will not do so in the presence of what is fashioned by man. I will go into the mountains and let it kill me before the face of God."

He and Ellen threw a banquet of salads and roasts and wines for all their friends one clear evening in July and the next morning the two of them left for an extended camping trip in the vicinity of Lake Infrequent. Ellen returned alone one month later, notified the authorities, then came to see me.

"He took the canoe while I was asleep," she said. "He didn't leave any note. I thought he might come back. I waited two weeks."

She paused and looked down at the rug, at her slender brown fingers. "I know now what he meant the afternoon before when he mentioned something about only God knowing where the body of Moses was."

As far as I know, Ellen did not stop playing the game. I know I did not. Nor did either of us stop camping by Lake Infrequent, though we never went there together.

One August night I had just pitched my tent when there was a remarkable display of shooting stars, a true firefall. I got into my sleeping bag and lay outside of the tent and watched the sky for hours. I caught myself imagining how Arthur might have interpreted a shooting star in terms of God's personality. Then I had the sensation that he

6

was right beside me, playing the game, answering my challenge, only I was not able to make out his words. The sensation did not frighten me, but it did keep me awake half the night wondering if Arthur knew all the correct interpretations now, or whether, in light of his different perspective on God, he had to start all over playing a game that could never end.

2

Lorine Jennifer Dies

S he had decided when she was nine years old that she would die in the autumn because it was the gentlest of all the seasons. It had not been a decision made in haste nor one made after being punished by her parents. She had made it in the backyard while she watched a young poplar shiver, its small leaves clattering like coins in her jeans pockets. Her stuffed rabbit had been next to her at the moment of decision. She conceived of death as the two of them being let down into a hole in the earth to begin a long journey through a tunnel in the dark. Some of the journey would have to be made on hands and knees, she knew, and she realized that often the roots of trees and bushes would tangle in her hair and frighten her—she had seen such roots in animals' burrows in the woods. Nevertheless, all of this would be worth it. For at the end of that tunnel would be a land of sun and red snapdragons and rolling fields of tall green grass. And if you died in autumn then that land would stay autumn for you forever, the leaves of poplar and the birch and the maple and the oak always yellow and orange and red and spotted. And all the persons who had died in the autumn would be waiting for you and there would be a picnic with large cookies and small green pickles.

God, she thought to herself, the garbage you can dream up when you're a kid. Then she smiled. In the pale glass of the window where the sun had just set her face smiled back so that it was like a grimace. Lorine Jennifer had been a good kid. But now she was Lorine Jennifer the adult, and it was the adult who was dying, and Lorine Jennifer the adult had not wanted to die at anytime, least of all in autumn with its splotches and globs of cheerful paint. It was like dying in the middle of the circus parade, dying among the red-nosed, orange-haired clowns.

Autumn was one time of year Lorine Jennifer felt like living, like starting over. She made resolutions in October the way some persons make them on New Year's Eve. A year ago in the fall she had felt particularly strong about the changes she was going to make in her life. It had been October sixth that she had written her resolutions down on the back of a cigarette package with a ballpoint that kept skipping. On October seventh friends had taken her to a downtown clinic and on October eighth a doctor on call had told her she had AIDS. The year had clawed at her throat and her body like sharp black November branches, and now, in her final autumn, the resolutions didn't matter anymore.

She shrugged, withdrew a cigarette from her lips, blew out a chunk of smoke. If the doctor had expected to see her cry, he sure got a surprise. She had stared back at him without moving a muscle and had said, "Is that all?" Leaving the clinic she had suddenly remembered a morning when she had been sitting cross-legged in a posh apartment, sunlight dropping off her face and hair, and she had felt so good, and the needle had felt so good, and to think, of all the dirty places she had shot up, it could have been in that two thousand-a-month penthouse suite that was cleaned three times a week by a maid. She had laughed out loud in front of the receptionist. A life full of jokes.

Her mother hustled into the hospital room, a heavy woman with dark hair and no sense of humour.

"Those nurses!" she rumbled. "They don't have anything else to do and they can't even see to it that you get your meals on time."

"The nurses have been great, Mom," Lorine Jennifer said. "Why don't you sit down and let them do their work?"

"Are you feeling all right, Jenn? Do you want some juice? I can go down to the drink machine and get you a can of cold juice."

"No, Mother, I'm not thirsty."

"It's no trouble. The machine's just down the hall."

"No, Mother. I'm fine."

"I'll just be a minute. Do you want orange or apple?"

"It doesn't matter. Apple."

Her mother and father had divorced when Lorine Jennifer was twelve or thirteen. At first she had seen both of them a lot even though she had lived with her mother. But when she started using drugs and getting into trouble with the police, her father had told her he didn't want to see her again until she smartened up. That never happened. Heroin was her life. She had convinced herself that the day would come when she would sign herself into a drug rehab centre and emerge pristine and sparkling, his princess once again. It had been one of her October sixth resolutions. She pulled her knees into her chest. His absence had always bothered her. For twenty years she hadn't been able to shake it. He had read to her all the time when she was a young girl. *The Velveteen Rabbit* had been their favourite. The memory of his body smell of Palmolive soap and pipe tobacco and white bread made her think of warm blankets, of windows shut tight against the winter, of lamps being turned off and a good darkness whirling like water. Her brothers and sisters had dropped by with cards that she had set up along the windowsill as though it were Christmas. But he had not come.

Her mother returned with a green can and a straw. Lorine Jennifer put out her cigarette and sipped the cool liquid. Her mother's large hand smoothed back Lorine Jennifer's pale brown hair, passed over her freckles that were like flakes of rust.

"Are you hungry?" her mother asked her. "I ought to go down to the nurse's station again."

"No, Mother. I'm fine, really. I don't have much of an appetite. Why don't you go and get yourself something to eat?"

"There's plenty of time for me to eat later. I'm here to see you. How are you feeling right now?"

"Not bad. Mom, do you think Dad will visit me?"

Her mother glanced quickly at the cards on the windowsill. "I don't know. You remember what he's like."

"Does he know I'm in here?"

"I'll call him tonight."

"Mom? I don't want you to tell him."

"What do you mean?"

"I don't want you to tell him I'm in the hospital."

"Why not?"

"I want him to think I'm still living downtown. I want him to look me up. I want my landlady to tell him where I am. I want him to come to me on his own."

"That man. Jennifer, he will never come to you on his own."

"Mom, please don't call him."

"Why can't I call him? Maybe he would come to see you now that you're in here."

"Because he might not come, Mother. He might not come even if you called him and told him I'm here. And I couldn't handle that."

A kind of ripping went through Lorine Jennifer's chest and into her stomach. She began to cry and she could not get her breath. She gasped and vomited and cried harder. Her mother went shrieking down the hall for a nurse.

I am going to die, thought Lorine Jennifer. I am going to die and he still won't come and see me. She bent over in bed. She felt sharp points prick her arms. My God, my father is not going to come and see me even though I'm dying.

The nurses calmed her, changed her bed linen, made her comfortable. She thanked them, her mother hovering off behind the nurses like a hail storm. She ate very little from her supper tray though her mother tried to coax her. Eventually, she fell asleep. She woke smelling her mother's perfume. It was midnight and her mother's chair was empty. She must have left for home. Lorine Jennifer maneuvered her IV pole to the washroom, then stumbled back to bed. Her stomach muscles ached. She sat in her bed looking at the dark pane of glass that was cold to the touch. She was going to die and be just as cold, colder. Winter.

When she was two she had walked in on her father urinating and had decided she wanted to go to the bathroom the same way Daddy did. No one, not even her father, could talk her out of trying to imitate him. For an entire week she had stubbornly persisted. But she had not been very successful and in the end she had given up and gone back to sitting on the toilet seat, though not without a fit of crying to cover up her anger and her shame. Then her father had told her a secret: He sometimes went to the bathroom the same way she did! And that had made her feel wonderful. God, he had been such a good father.

She woke at two, again at five. She was icy. She imagined her body in a coffin, being lowered into the earth. No tunnel, the coffin landed on mud and rock with a solid thud. She pulled the cord of the call light for the nurse. The woman who came in was young and small and gentle, like the tiny poplar.

"What's wrong, Lorine?"

"I don't know. Is there a chaplain here or anything?"

"A chaplain?"

"It doesn't have to be a priest. A minister, someone I can talk to."

"I'm sorry, Lorine. This hospital doesn't have a chaplain. Is there a minister I can call for you? A family minister?"

"No. I guess not. Mom would know. Can't you call anyone for me?"

"I can find someone. Does it matter what denomination the minister belongs to?"

"I don't know. Look, it's morning now. The sun's coming up. It can wait. I feel better."

"Are you sure, Lorine? It's no problem. I can just pick up the phone."

"No, no thanks. I feel better. It's light now. If I change my mind, I'll let you know."

Church. Tiny white shoes, a purse, a blue dress. Her father had walked her in his black suit and hat. She cut out pictures of lambs and Jesus holding them. She couldn't remember her mother going to church. No one went when she was a teenager. Once she had started doing drugs and was on the street she would sit and smoke and listen to the street preachers and sometimes take their tracts. She always considered herself more religious than the other street people, but the groups that came downtown from churches in the suburbs, their guitars shiny and their hair combed and their clothes ironed, they only made her laugh. They tried to be so with it, tried to imitate the street jargon whenever they spoke, and it was all so put on, so fake, she would get up and walk, taking a tract and ripping it up right in front of them.

The only time anyone had ever gotten to her was on a Friday night in November, maybe a month before Christmas. A bunch of men and women in their fifties were on a corner singing old hymns. No guitars, no teenagers to stand there and tell everyone how Jesus had got them off drugs. Just these parent-types in long brown coats and hats singing, "Jesus saves, Jesus saves," and a man who could have been her father quietly smiling, hopeful, offering long white tracts, flushing when rebuffed, but still trying to smile, still trying to give. Lorine had gone up to him, taken all his tracts, and had handed them out to all the street people, made each person take one. Then one of the church men, small and slender with a moustache like a line of charcoal, stepped forward and swept off his hat and pleaded with them all to give their lives to Jesus. He kept extending his arm with his hat at the end of it. A beggar begging them for their lives. He only spoke for a minute or two in a loud voice and then he stopped and five or six of the others began to sing another hymn, their voices high and cracking in the cold night. Lorine Jennifer looked at them, the women with their black-buttoned coats and their dark hair pinned up in buns under their hats, struggling to read the words to the hymn under the street lamp, and she began to cry. She came up and sagged into one of the women's arms and kept crying while the woman patted her on the back. She said a prayer with the man who looked like her father, took the address of their little church, promised to join them Sunday morning, never went, never saw any of them again.

Her mother arrived immediately after breakfast with a basket of black purple grapes, the kind Lorine Jennifer enjoyed the most.

"Thanks, Mom. They taste great."

"Go ahead. Have some more."

"No, that's enough. I'll eat some more later. I just had breakfast."

"Go ahead. They didn't cost me anything. Do you want something to drink?"

"No, I'm fine now. Thanks, Mom."

"How did you sleep last night?"

"Okay. Mom, do we have a family minister?"

"A family minister? What do you want to know that for?"

"Do we have one?"

"We used to have one. Nobody's been to church for years, not since your sister Karyn was married. Why do you want to know?"

"I'd like to talk to a minister, that's all. Could you call up the minister who married Karyn for me?"

"Why don't you talk to the minister here?"

"They don't have one. I asked the nurse."

"That doesn't surprise me, the way this hospital is run. When do you want me to tell the minister to come?"

"After supper. Around sunset. That would be the best time."

"All right. I'll call him now. Can I get you anything from the cafeteria? A muffin?"

"No thanks, Mom. I'm stuffed."

"What kind of muffin do you want?"

"I don't want one. Blueberry, if they have it."

Lorine Jennifer dozed off and on throughout the day. The window became a kind of silent movie screen for her. There was a school near the hospital and she watched the children walking to and from it, watched them coiling on the monkey bars in the playground and tumbling down the gleaming slide. A boy threw cranberry-coloured leaves at two blonde girls in denim overalls. Her father used to rake the leaves into a huge mound and then toss her brothers and sisters into it. She would be the last and he always tossed her in after swinging her upside down. An enormous battle would ensue, leaves ending up down backs, inside shirts and underwear, crackling into flakes and chips in everyone's hair. Her father would attempt to stop the battle after about ten minutes but no one would listen to him. They would turn on him in a bunch and pin him down and stuff leaves into every opening they could find, particularly his mouth.

Each colour through the window was sharp and distinct as if freshly applied to the earth. She gazed as the wind tickled a willow, so that one moment the tree shone like brass and the next moment the thin leaves had been flipped and glimmered like nickels. The blue over the trees was thick and swirling. She slept, woke, slept. The blue lasted forever. Yet finally she opened her eyes and noticed a change in the texture of the light. The earth's colours were being muted. She thought of a story: Night is arriving with hat and cane, whisking the long tail of his dark cloak down the ballroom of the sky. Lorine Jennifer felt weak, sensed her bowels loosening, barely made it to the washroom.

When she returned and sagged into her bed, the window pane was black.

She picked at her supper, her mother left to go to a meeting, the nurse bent over her, like autumn, like the tiny poplar, asking her if she needed anything. Lorine Jennifer said she was doing pretty good, that she was expecting their family minister at any time. She waited, turned on the bedside lamp, said nothing when one of her IV bags was replaced. At nine o'clock she pulled on the call light and asked the nurse if she wouldn't mind telephoning the minister and asking him how much longer he would be. His number was on a slip of paper by her ice water jug. The nurse promised to call right away, took the paper and moved off down the hall to the nurses' station. She rang up the minister and informed him that Lorine Jennifer had been expecting him for some time. The minister apologized, said he had been tied up with church business, that he would come down to see Lorine Jennifer some time in the morning. The nurse insisted that Lorine Jennifer needed to see him tonight.

"I'm very tired," said the minister. "Surely tomorrow morning will be all right. It's not an emergency, is it?"

"She could lapse into a coma at any time, sir," the nurse told him.

"Well, I'm sure it will keep till morning. I'm not a great believer in deathbed conversions anyhow."

After the nurse had hung up, she sat alone in the nurses' station for about five minutes. The others were all with their patients and an orderly had come by to help with turning several of the heavier patients over on their sides. She tried to think of a good way to tell Lorine Jennifer the minister was not coming.

The nurse had been raised in a Christian home herself but God and her had fallen on hard times in recent years. When she had been a teenager her prayers had seemed to soar to God, now they wilted a foot from her mouth and she pictured God as a huge wall the colour of plaster. She attended church services whenever her erratic shift work permitted but these also blotted out God, made him into a formal, middle-class North American with suit, tie, and business concerns. Now she was scrambling—for, in fact, it mattered to her that God was hidden, lost, absent. She wanted to see him, feel some emotions over him, sense that when she prayed some kind of communication was taking place.

There was a small Bible in her purse which she carried about with her. She had made a resolution to read it during her lunch breaks, hoping to regenerate some sort of spiritual vitality within herself. But the biblical words had stuck together like clumps of clay and she had bogged down in familiar passages she had read hundreds of times before. They evoked unpleasant sensations of being sixteen, sitting in Sunday School, and the whole world moving along perfectly like a white-faced electric clock. She dug the white book from her green leather bag anyway. Someone had to do something for Lorine Jennifer. She walked briskly to the room.

The minister would be late. Would Lorine Jennifer like to look at a Bible? Lorine Jennifer shrugged. She found herself a cigarette, asked the nurse if she cared to talk for a bit, sat forward in bed, her knees at her chin.

Sometimes the night was busy for the nurse, sometimes it was not. When there was time, the two women talked. They crouched on the bed like two teenage girls at a sleepover, whispered, covered their mouths when they laughed, clutched each other's arms and raised their voices when common ground was suddenly discovered. Each time enthusiasm increased, sentences became shorter and simpler, they spoke with an innocence and a boldness, as if they were childhood confidants. Lorine Jennifer talked a great deal about her father, the nurse quite a bit about her own mother. Both agreed that God would have to be a God sort of like Lorine Jennifer's father and the nurse's mother. God would have to be able to laugh, to dance, to rub whiskers against your face, to roll you around in a pile of leaves, to roast potatoes under a bonfire and pull them out just when they were black and hot and good. God would have to be able to play games with you and throw you up in the air and catch you, never missing. Not only that, God would have to be able to listen to everything you told him, whether it was serious or make-believe, and not scorn it or get bored. God would have to be able to keep secrets. God would have to be tolerant of your mistakes and not lecture you all the time about them—God would have to let you make a mess of things now and again. In short, they both decided, God would have to let you be a kid. If God could do that, then there was hope for the two of them.

The nurse left for home shortly after dawn, tugging on her sweater and riding the elevator down to the main floor. The two young women had hugged and had told each other they were looking forward to speaking again during the nurse's next set of shifts in four days' time. The nurse found the air unusually rich with the scent of grass and frost and walked towards the sun where she had parked her car. She crunched through the brown and brittle leaves in the gutter as she unlocked the driver's door.

Lorine Jennifer hauled her IV pole to the washroom, washed her face, and climbed back into bed. The window pane was throwing light across her sheets. She prayed while she smoked one of her last two cigarettes, said good morning when her mother walked in, drank only the orange juice on her breakfast tray. The minister did not show up, Lorine Jennifer said nothing about it to her mother. They passed the day reminiscing about relatives. For supper Lorine Jennifer drank the apple juice and nibbled on a piece of brown bread. Her mother scolded her, went looking for a nurse and complained they weren't feeding her daughter enough of the right food. When the room became dark with night, Lorine Jennifer tensed her stomach muscles, breathed in and out slowly and carefully, put the Bible the nurse had left under the pillow, and fell asleep with her face turned towards the window. It rained all the next day until evening and she felt soaked through and chilled. She sipped tea at various hours. Her mother left a box of Turtles and she ate half of it. She prayed once again, in the dark, watching the red end of her cigarette, and thought of her father smoking a pipe in front of the fireplace on Saturday nights. He would stare into the burning slabs of pine and maple and she would watch him stare and puff and she thought the smell of his pipe tobacco the most wonderful smell in the world. She would lie against his side and his arm would fall over neck and shoulders and stomach. "Father," she said. "God," she said.

Lorine Jennifer was charted by a flow nurse as having expired at 0430 hours. Her mother and brothers and sisters came and gazed at her, white face in white pillow and white sheets. After the family had left the nurses wrapped up the body in a white plastic shroud, tying a white tag to her large toe and binding her hands together at the wrist and crossing them over her breasts. An orderly arrived with a stainless steel trolley and they placed the body on its lower rack and covered the trolley with a huge white sheet so that only hospital staff would know a body was there. The orderly rolled the trolley past the nurse's station where four or five nurses were rushing about getting ready for the day's work. The telephone rang and Emergency was sending a new patient up to take Lorine Jennifer's bed. A nurse ran to make the bed over with fresh linen and wipe the bedframe with antiseptic. The orderly and a nurse took an elevator down to the morgue where they transferred Lorine Jennifer's body onto a smaller trolley which they pushed into a room of cold air. It had a door like a refrigerator. There were four other trolleys in the room all holding neatly wrapped white bundles. The orderly and nurse went out and shut the door and washed their hands with a yellow liquid soap at a nearby sink. Then the orderly dried his hands on his pants and rode the elevator up a floor where he got off and walked out of the front doors of the hospital to get a breath of fresh air. A blizzard of bright leaves blinded him, made him cover his eyes with a hand and look away.

3

The Body God

"What if God should come as a human?" asked the professor of comparative religions with a smile. "Would he come as a Buddhist, all serene and peaceful? Would he come as a Moslem, all fiery and zealous? Or would he come as a Christian—middle class and well-off and loaded down with creature comforts?"

🌺

Now Mary is in her final month of pregnancy. She is as big as a house. The baby in her womb kicks with little feet, punches out with tiny fists. God is anxious to get out and discover the human experience. At night Joseph places his ear to Mary's swollen stomach. How faint the heartbeat is, so faint, as if it were light years away. The Creator of the human race, growing human fingers and toes, submerged in human waters, nourished by human blood.

He could have been born in Nazareth in a warm room in a warm bed surrounded by family and friends, with a midwife to assist. Why did he make it so difficult for himself? Why did he make it so difficult for Mary? A hundred miles or more on a donkey, jerking up and down over the rocky paths, biting her lip, her womb so agitated by the journey that by the time Joseph brings her into Bethlehem she has gone into labour.

And the town crammed with those who have come to register for the census, and the houses full of bright lights and noise and the loud laughter of parties and the loud voices of people who have had too much to drink, and strangers all around Mary, staring at her, leering at her, and she frightened and in pain. And rejected. At the inn, turned away. Until finally a cave carved out of a hillside, a stable, full of straw and manure and stink and animals seating and bellowing and stamping their feet in the evening chill.

So with the sound of fighting and drinking floating through the night air, Mary screams and bites the knotted cloth in her mouth and God erupts into Joseph's hands in a gush of water and blood. In her pain and exhaustion, Mary laughs, as humans always laugh after the same anguish and pain and struggle to discover God when suddenly, joyously, they are born a second time, finding to their surprise that God is so very simple, so down-to-earth, so near at hand. And Joseph laughing, with fatherhood and relief, severing the umbilical cord, cutting free a God of bone and hair and skin. The Body God, howling as he is cupped in huge human hands nicked with poverty, the blood being scrubbed from his head and hands and feet, his body being cleaned of human gore, not for the last time.

And suddenly a dozen filthy men crowd into the stable and Joseph seizes his knife, but they do nothing but stare, their faces white in the light of one small torch. Their eyes are wide, they look like they have just seen ghosts. Who will ever believe them? Maybe it was too much wine, too little sleep, but look, the baby is there after all.

What do they understand as they squat in the shiver of light? Do they see God clinging to a woman's breast for sustenance? Is it God they hear wailing into the cold dark? Thirty years later when the child wails down the long cave of death, stretched to a cross, will they recognize him as the one angels told them to find?

At an icy grey dawn Joseph sits by his wife and his quiet child— after crying most of the night, God has decided to have his first sleep. The stable boy comes in to feed the livestock and is startled to find Joseph and Mary there and a baby snoring in a feeding trough. Cursing and yelling at them for being vagrants, he throws them out. The baby wakes and begins to cry again, but Mary comforts him at her breast. Joseph places his arm around her and helps her back into Bethlehem.

There is no one to greet them and the town is as still as death.

Practically everyone is hung over from the parties of the night before. Mary wraps God snugly against the cold and the three of them go from door to door. No one will respond to their knocking. Someone yells down at them: "Go away!"

But a Body God cannot vanish into thin air.

4

The Professor's Theophany

Robert Bodey, PhD, was growing weary of theology. He had been teaching it for twenty-five years and he was bored. So he gained weight. His usually impeccable apartment became a shambles. He avoided returning to it for as long as possible after work because he felt lonely in it—there was only the furniture, a small TV, and wall after wall of huge books with German titles stamped on their spines, all now in disarray. He stopped changing the sheets on his bed too. They became itchy and grey with granules of dirt.

Robert Bodey was not married. He had planned to get a PhD and he had gotten a PhD. He had planned to get a position at a university teaching theology and he had gotten a position at a university teaching theology. But he had not planned to get a marriage, so he did not have one of those. He was a bachelor. At fifty-five he frequented an inexpensive Chinese restaurant for his meals or ate Hamburger Helper and Rice-a-roni out of the pots he cooked them in.

After a year in this depressed state he decided to have a physician he knew look him over. The doctor didn't even bother to use his stethoscope.

"You're fat," the doctor said. "You look like one of the pyramids of Egypt. I want you to find a dog for yourself and get out every morning for some exercise."

Bodey reflected and decided to get two dogs. He chose them from the other side of the glass pane while both of the puppies were sleeping—he concluded from this that they were a quiet breed of dog. They turned his apartment into a racetrack and then, with unabated energy, a wrestling ring. He proceeded to take his first walk immediately, following the doctor's orders with commendable alacrity, nursing a vain hope of tiring the two puppies out.

Bodey lived in a small apartment block just off campus. The university owned hundreds of acres of forested land which it had not yet developed and this land was interlaced with trails. People walked on them, jogged on them, cycled on them. Bodey turned his two puppies loose on them and strolled behind them at a moderate pace. The puppies would race ahead, peer about for Bodey's triangular hulk and elfish legs, run back to him, jump on him, then race ahead once more. Bodey spent an hour in this fashion every day and in time, surprising himself, he came to enjoy it. And the puppies brought life into his apartment also, made it something of a home. After six months Bodey did begin to lose weight, found he could breathe better, and he began to laugh when he lectured, which startled his students, who thought he was choking.

Despite all these physical and psychological improvements, however, the puppies were unable to do anything about Bodey's general malaise towards his teaching career. The new red and yellow hardbacked tomes in his office, sent gratis by various publishers, remained unopened. He no longer revised his lecture notes from one semester to the next. He eventually came to the point where he seriously began to consider some kind of dramatic exit from the whole farce, as he had come to view it. Perhaps crying STRAW! in the middle of a lecture on God's self-revelation to the human race, walking out, plugging the toilets in the washrooms with pages from his theology books, and then resigning. He actually decided on this particular course of action, set the date five months in advance, and stolidly awaited its arrival. In the meantime, he continued to walk his puppies, who were now truly dogs, and to look at the green of the trees as he briskly strode past them down one trail after another.

Two weeks after he had made the decision to end his career as a theologian, a woman with a black Labrador Retriever stopped to chat with him on a trail. She admired his two dogs.

"Are these Malamutes?" she asked.

"Yes," answered Bodey, who wasn't sure what she meant.

"They have a beautiful wild look to them."

"They do, don't they?"

"Did you know there were coyotes in these woods here?"

"Pardon me?"

"Coyotes. A whole pack of them. They've been here for years."

"Coyotes?" exclaimed Bodey. "Coyotes in the middle of the third largest city in the country? That's hard to believe."

The woman shrugged. "Well, they're here. Miles and miles of forest for them. I saw the pack once. That would be two years ago now."

"You couldn't have been mistaken?" probed Bodey. "You're sure you weren't seeing a German Shepherd or something?"

The woman laughed at him. "Oh, no. These weren't German Shepherds. They have quite a different look to them. Quite a different way of moving. Very wild. Feral. You can't mistake them for somebody's pet."

After this surprising conversation, Bodey took it upon himself to casually ask other dog owners he met on the trails if they had heard of the coyotes. Some of them had, some of them didn't know what he was talking about, and a few claimed they had seen them with their own eyes. Their sightings tended to be brief, perhaps only a glimpse of a lean figure loping through swordferns, but one or two declared the coyotes had shadowed them, quietly keeping pace with them and their dogs. Coyotes were killers, a man said. A bitch would lure a dog into the woods where another coyote, her partner, would get in behind the dog, hamstring it, and then both would gobble it up. The man warned Bodey to keep his dogs on a leash if he ever saw anything suspicious, and then remarked on the coyotes's sinister amber eyes. "A lot like the wolf," the man assured him. Others spoke of the beauty of the coyotes, their wonderful coats and their huge bushy tails, their sleek forms and the grace with which they moved through the rain forest. "They're very shy, very timid," these persons explained to Bodey. "Not at all like the wolf."

Bodey sensed a growing desire within him to see these coyotes for himself. Some of the curiosity, he knew, had to do with the fact that, like most city-dwellers, the only wild animals he had ever seen had been behind bars, which hardly made them wild, or they had been making fools of themselves in national or provinicial parks, begging for white bread and potato chips. How many times did you see a wild animal in its natural environment? He was aware that people who lived in the midst of coyotes and bears and wolves all their lives, ranchers and farmers up north, for instance, could get so used to seeing them they practically ignored the creatures—unless they viewed them as intruders and nuisances that threatened their livestock and needed to be poisoned, trapped or shot. But Bodey was in a state of almost childlike wonder, wanting to see a wild animal, to look into its eyes without wire or gun between it and him, with no desire on his part to do anything but gaze and perhaps—he only mentioned this to his dogs—talk to it.

Accordingly, he began to gather information from those who had seen the coyotes about where they had seen them and at what time of day. When some of them wanted to know why and he told them he hoped to see the coyotes for himself, a few smiled and encouraged him, but others said, "You don't want to see them. They'll give you the creeps. The bunch of them will circle around you. We don't understand enough about coyotes to know what they'd do to a person if they got him alone."

Bodey could not deny having a few garish daydreams of sprawling in a thicket with his throat torn open while he watched a coyote chew on his leg and thigh, but the excitement of the quest was overpowering. He went to all the locations in the forest where people claimed they had seen the coyotes and he went at every different time of day imaginable. He even went at night once, a flashlight in his pocket, when the calls of the birds and the creaking of the tree limbs made him think of films he'd seen about Vietnam.

When he had no luck, he went to the university library and read up on coyotes' habits. Apparently, he would have a better chance of catching a sight of them just before dawn. So he began leaping out of bed at five every morning and hauling his bewildered dogs out onto the trails, his eyes scanning the trees around him, his ears alert to the slightest rustling sound. Once, after a rain, he thought the sound of fat raindrops plopping off the trees into the undergrowth was the padding of coyote paws through the ferns. Another time he followed a set of wolfish tracks down a muddy, skinny trail that led off a larger one into the densest sections of the forest. He tripped over roots, hauled his body over huge cedar deadfalls, soaked his feet in black puddles, scraped his face on thorns. At the end of the path the tracks stopped under the paws of a Siberian Husky which had stopped to urinate against a tree while its master lit a cigarette.

Despite the fact that he heard nothing and saw nothing, Bodey kept hoping, though his earlier zest faded. He stopped getting up at five. The strong leashes he had purchased for the dogs in preparation for the encounter with the coyotes he frequently left behind in the apartment. As the months passed, he thought less of the coyotes and more of his disillusionment with his profession. The only times of day he looked forward to now were his hours with his dogs and the moment he turned off the light to go to sleep. He returned the books on coyotes he had assembled back to the university library and he did not renew them. Everyone who mentioned sighting the coyotes was talking about an experience they had had two or three years before. Bodey reasoned that the pack had moved on, had stolen past the city limits to the mountains where they belonged.

Two days before his planned dramatic resignation, the clocks went ahead one hour because of daylight saving time. Bodey dutifully reset the hands of his wristwatch and alarm clock and went to bed thinking of how he would fling the word STRAW! at those serious men and women scratching their notes about God into their binders of foolscap. He rehearsed the moment again and again, lost consciousness, dreamed about nothing. He got up at six, dressed, and took the dogs on the trails.

It had been raining, but the sky was a light spring grey, not the grim charcoal of the winter months, and the silver light brightened the green around him. He did not feel much like walking and wanted to get it over with, hurrying the dogs along, becoming impatient with them if they dawdled too long in a particular pool or at a particular odour. His pace slowed and his head went down as he thought about his Monday morning lecture. Just to get it over and done with and to get out, never to look back. Why had he ever wanted to study theology in the first place? The lifeless abstractions, the predictable conclusions, the vague and drawn-out analyses of the divine. Perhaps he could get a job at the post office.

An old man with an iron-coloured moustache, black beret, brown walking stick, and two large German Shepherds came briskly up the path towards him.

"Morning," grunted Bodey.

"A big noise in the bush," the old man said. "I think there are coyotes back in there."

Bodey grunted again. A tree falling. Birds. Most likely a squirrel or racoon. Bodey passed on with his dogs and his eyes reverted to the dirt and stones just ahead of the toes of his shoes.

The cry startled him. He knew immediately what it was not. it was not a dog. The cry came again, around a swerve in the trail, partly a bark, partly a wail. Bodey stopped to listen. Again it came, louder and closer. The dogs milled about his feet, confused, whining. Then there were two cries, answering each other, high, with a dying twist to them. An instant later and there was a powerful burst of yipping and howling. My God, thought Bodey, my God. He began to run. The dogs ran with him.

Each half-minute or so he stopped running, listened, gauged his distance from the sounds. After a couple of minutes he was right on top of the cries, they were breaking out of the forest off to his left. The leashes were in his pocket. Fumbling with the catches, he snapped them onto the dogs' collars. They plunged into the woods, stumbling over branches and moss-covered stumps. Far from the trail, Bodey stopped again, his heart bumping against his chest, his breath loud, a pant leg ripped open. A cry shot at him from a clump of pine twenty feet away. He squinted, strained to see, knew it was there, saw only pine needles and thin, grey tree trunks. The dogs hurled themselves forward, almost tearing their leashes free from his tight grip. They ran behind him, leaped forward again, so that the leashes bound them-selves around Bodey's legs and he fell, his mouth filling with dirt and chips of rotten cedar. He untangled himself and got up and spat. The calls came from farther away. They were leaving.

Bodey cried out, tried to imitate the call, yipped, howled, fought to put a quaver in his voice. A cry responded to his. He howled again, his dogs churning up the moss at his feet, twisting him around with their leashes, pawing at the air. Yowls and barks were fired back at Bodey from the woods. The dogs jumped ahead and Bodey fell back-wards into a deadfall. The broken end of a branch punctured his shoul-der. Another cry, still farther away, a note at the end of it, as if it were asking a question, hanging there in the green and in the polished sil-ver. Bodey struggled up, howled, had both leashes in one fist, began to run deeper into the woods. Wails answered him from behind a distant cedar stump as wide and high as a small hill. He and the dogs blun-dered towards it. When they reached the monstrous stump, there was nothing, but the dogs sniffed it vigorously and Bodey felt eyes on him, thought he saw a face and ears, no, only another stump, stood as still as he could, praying, squinting, wanting. Nothing. There were no more cries.

He and the dogs found their way out of the forest, got back on one of the main trails. He unfastened the dogs' leashes and they raced off into the bars of yellow light, the sun wedging its way in-between two clouds. Right away they met a man with a springer spaniel.

"Coyotes," Bodey panted. "Did you hear the coyotes?"

"No," the man replied.

"Back there in the woods. They were almost singing to each other."

The man called to his spaniel: "Come on, Tina, come on, girl. Nice meeting you."

The man moved along the trail. But Bodey had to talk. He met a woman and a man with their collie. He forced himself to observe the usual amenities. Then he told them he had been right on top of the coyotes, that they had been howling all around him.

"You know," responded the man, "I heard them two or three years ago. But I haven't heard them since."

"Just over there." Bodey gestured. "Just off that trail. Calling and yipping."

"Well, that's interesting. That's very interesting. I would have thought they'd have moved on by now."

The three of them listened but heard only the stirring of branches, a robin. The couple smiled at Bodey.

"We'll push on," they said. "Nice talking to you."

Bodey was out early the next morning, and the next, but heard nothing, saw nothing. He walked off the trails, stumbled through the bush with his dogs on leash. He sat quietly near huge stumps and waited. The light would break and fall on his shoulders and head.

He continued to mention what had happened to the other dog owners he met on the trail. Some listened and said nothing. Others changed the subject. Once he spoke about it at a faculty meeting and a colleague of his puffed at his pipe and snorted, "Coyotes? Coyotes in the middle of the third largest city in the country? That's hard to believe." Another laughed. "Well, you know, I've seen them. I've seen them back there. That was years ago. But it's a lot different when you get a look at them. They're kind of scrawny creatures, actually."

31

Bodey did not leave the university. He did throw out most of his notes and extensively revised all his lectures. He often spoke extemporaneously, sometimes rambled. It was impossible to get rid of him because of his tenure. His classes dwindled. Students claimed they saw him wandering, apparently aimlessly, through the woods with his two dogs and they chuckled. The story even went around that he had been seen walking through the trees and howling like a wolf or coyote.

Yet a nucleus of students became devoted to him, attending all his lectures, asking questions, producing thoughtful and penetrating essays. One young woman came up with an award-winning thesis, astonishing the faculty. How did Bodey's meanderings and mumbo-jumbo, they demanded, inspire such leanness of prose, such blazing insight, such astounding intimacy with the divine? "As if," one professor remarked, "the lot of them had gone on a hike with the Almighty."

Bodey made no comments to anyone, did not involve himself in any of the controversy or faculty intrigue. He went back and forth along obscure trails that curled in and out of the rain forest, his dogs leaping ahead, he striding behind, stopping to listen, pausing to squint through the bristling green, often leaving the trail and struggling to make his own path through branches and swordfern and rot. These explorations became the very stuff of his life, and you would find him sitting on a stump with his hands just under his nose, eyes focused straight ahead, for all the world like something that had grown up out of the rain forest itself, palms together, thinking God knows what.

5

Boj

N ow there was a man named Boj. Boj is Job spelt backwards and that is what his father, a religious man, had him christened, much as other families will name their children after Bible heroes such as David, Jonathan, Deborah, and Rachel, or after the apostles of Jesus. There was, for instance, on the same block that Boj grew up on, a Spanish family that had named their daughter Immaculate Conception. Such people hope that giving their children biblical names will perhaps infuse them with some of those characters' better qualities or, at the very least, that God will smile upon such children and deal more congenially with them, guiding them through the pitfalls and temptations that destroy so many parents' dreams. This was the hope of Boj's father, for he was a frightened, superstitious believer in the Christ, whom he considered capricious, and he hoped that by spelling Job's name backwards and bestowing it upon his son, all of Job's bad fortune would be reversed in the child's life.

As a matter of fact, the name caused more grief for the child in his public school years instead of the hoped-for reverse. Other children not only ridiculed him and made up the kind of brutal rhymes that only children are capable of creating, but teachers often joined in the mockery too, either inadvertently through mispronunciation of his name, or deliberately, but slyly, when they wished to see another creature suffer as they were suffering trying to teach their callous and disobedient pupils.

Despite all this, or probably because of it, Boj grew up very quiet and very tender, sensitive to others' pains and needs. He became a junior high teacher, and he taught English, and he taught it well. His students loved him, for he loved them first. Often he became dramatic in the classroom, acting out scenes from the novels and plays they studied together. Many a boy or girl, hearing and watching him, felt their image pierced and laughter come, or anguish, and sometimes a tear forced inward to be released and shed in a dark, starry backyard, hands in pockets, lonely and hoping for a voice from the black mystery of two o'clock in the morning.

And despite his father, his name, and the dubious blessing it had brought upon his head, Boj came to love God. He attended a small church irregularly, listened to the sermons, remained quiet and smiled when others shouted praise. But in his own home, when no one else was with him, he would read the Bible out loud dramatically, and act out many of the events contained within its pages: Jesus before the tomb of Lazarus, Paul facing the council at Jerusalem, Jonah screaming out of the belly of a great fish, Elijah trekking to Mount Sinai and huddling in a cave to wait for the whisper of God. Then he would be overcome with joy and pain, and his face would flood with tears, and he would dance, dance in circles and fling up his arms, dance from living room to kitchen to bedroom to dining room, dance until the sweat washed away the tears, dance until he could hardly breathe and the laughter was erupting from him like the chiming of silver stars colliding happily with each other in the heavens. He would collapse on the floor on his back, still laughing, looking up at the panting, laughing face of God, his only partner, and he would begin to talk with him. This could go on for hours and often Boj merely fell asleep on the floor where he had collapsed, his round face still as a child's, his brown hair clinging damp where it grew around his ears and the back of his head, his bald scalp tinted rose by the flush of blood to his face, his arms spread-eagled.

The teenagers in the church desperately wanted him to be their youth pastor, but the senior minister would not allow it, and the adults in the church agreed with his decision. It was not that Boj wasn't a decent, God-fearing man, they each assured one another, but he was a little odd, and he frequently said things that bothered you for days afterwards, and he never worshipped as the others in the church did.

Besides, he was not regular in attendance and was certainly a bit too chummy with the non-Christian community. He was not altogether a very religious man, when all was said and done, and they could hardly allow such a man, decent and God-fearing though he was, to have such a position of responsibility over their children, whom they had named David and Jonathan and Deborah and Rachel.

All this Boj knew. He only smiled sadly and continued to teach his classes in English, and to dance in his home, and to dress simply and eat simply—he was somewhat poor since he sent the greater part of his paycheque to an invalid sister.

But he did not complain, nor shake his fist at heaven, nor curse God, though he was often hurt and perplexed. He did not rebel against the laughing God who was his only dancing partner.

An uncle Boj had never heard of finally called in his lawyer and settled his will in a hospital bed in-between coughing up blood and a nurse sliding a tube down his throat and sucking up brown and yellow phlegm. He named Boj as his sole beneficiary, inasmuch as the uncle was a religious man who had made his fortune in munitions and nuclear warheads, and who, having heard of Boj's piety from another nephew, hoped this gift of all the money he had ever earned from all the wars he had ever supplied, would appease God with regard to his feet swift to shed blood. After all, the money was going to one who was definitely God's child and who, in accordance with his faith, would use the money, very likely, to advance the kingdom of God upon the earth.

A day after his signing of this will, the uncle was alone in his private hospital room. Looking out the window he saw the evening shadows glide into the room together, from trees and houses and people, and congeal into the sharp outline of a long, thin darkness. He summoned up his act of bestowing his money on a child of God and awaited the peace which ought to accompany this summons. None came. An arm that seemed the concentration of all the darkness since the earth's beginning, so dense it was, spilled rapidly towards him like ink from a smashed bottle. He tried to cry out as his soul was slashed open and his life fled from him.

When a nurse entered the room it was full of the night. As she shone her flashlight towards the bed, she saw the slack jaw and the bulging eyes, and the first two fingers of her right hand came automatically and professionally to close the eyelids down over the screaming gaze.

35

Boj was rich.

He did not want to move from his house, but so many of his family pressed him to do so he finally acquiesced, both to please them and to escape the hundreds of people he'd never known who were continually dropping by day and night.

All of these people knew what to do with his money. A hundred missions groups came by, a thousand Christian businessmen. They plagued him constantly, like locusts. They raised their voices to God because of the blessing he had bestowed on Boj. They thanked God that Boj was considered righteous enough to receive it. All the voices said the same thing, no voice said anything to the contrary, so that Boj had to struggle to keep from believing it himself. Though he knew his God could not be so easily manipulated by his children's actions, whether to blessings or cursings, the voices were incessant. He thought he would lose his mind. He prayed but received no response. Eventually, he had no time to pray at all and hardly any time alone in which to dance.

His new house was located in a plush area of town and most of his neighbours were lawyers, doctors, and assorted corporation executives. They considered him an eccentric whom they rarely saw except when he was going to and from school in his white, open-neck shirt and dishevelled brown slacks. Soon they did not even see him then, for the principal asked him to conclude his year at Christmas. Boj's teaching and the manner in which he had been able to hold his students spell-bound had fallen far below par.

For the business of running his late uncle's empire was formidable indeed. Corporate lawyers, women representing buyers from countries he'd only read of in *Time*, men from the Department of National Defence, chief executives from the conglomerate's offices and munitions plants across the country, signatures, decisions, financial advisers to heed, document after document to read and consider.

Boj had refused to leave the new house and set up in his uncle's offices a thousand miles away, so they all came to him at his home. Soon he had to hire a dozen secretaries and bookkeepers and a number of household staff and a gardener. At first, he had abhorred the thought of carrying on with his uncle's business interests, considering what they were, and was about to close down the whole operation and distribute the capital to world relief organizations. But he met with an outpouring of protest from all those who heard about this plan, followers of the Christ and followers of anything but the Christ.

Men and women brutally reminded him of the mass unemployment this would cause, inaugurating possibly a national crisis; that the nation would lose the benefit of billions of dollars in armament sales so that the economy would sink even further, creating more suffering and swelling the ranks of the poor; that commitments had been made up to ten years in advance and that, in the name of all that was sacred and holy, these commitments had to be honoured. Boj had seen no way out of these implications and had reluctantly carried on with the business of running his inheritance. "Better you with your Christian principles," whispered a friend in his ear, "then, God forbid, someone else without them."

In all this, he did not forget God, nor did he stop dancing, though he had fewer opportunities and he danced with less and less conviction. Often he would stop in the middle of a dance and fall to his knees weeping because he did not mean the dance at all. No laughing God stooped over him, panting from dancing Boj's hora of worship. But Boj did not curse God, or rebel against him, or ignore him. Nor could he thank God once for the inheritance that had made him financally rich but spiritually poor.

A war escalated to a feverish pitch in his head. On the one hand, did not everything ultimately come from God's outstretched arm? Should God not be glorified and praised in all? On the other hand, was everything that came a person's way in life a blessing? Was not evil often mingled with good? Was God to be praised for all the wickedness in the world? How many Christians had Satan made wealthy who were adamant that their financial success came from God? How many churches grew because congregations thrived on the worship of Mammon which they could not distinguish any longer from the spirit of God? Witches, Satanists, all the cults held billions of dollars in assets. Which was the voice of the serpent? Which was the whisper of the dove?

"You're wrong!" one businessman cried, confronting Boj in his office. "You're completely off the wall not to praise God for this. Give thanks in all things, Boj. You're totally ignoring the hand of God in this. You're not giving him any of the credit due his name. You're sinning, Boj. And God punishes sin. He won't let his glory be trampled underfoot."

"Suppose this is a test, a trial," responded Boj, his face growing warm, "suppose this money is straight from the pit. How do you know God doesn't want me just to stand up and walk away from it?"

"Boj," said the senior minister of his little church, "a man of your spiritual acumen would be an asset to the leadership of our church. What happened to you convinced us you are a man who walks with God."

"I am the same man I always was," declared Boj, "the same man you wouldn't allow to be the church's youth pastor. I haven't changed, I never changed."

"Boj, you're a righteous man!" called another.

"I'm a sinner saved by grace," Boj retorted.

"Let us interview you," coaxed a Christian broadcaster. "You will give people hope. A little man in a little town with a little job, but he trusts and serves God quietly and faithfully. Finally, the day comes when that quiet faithfulness is rewarded. Don't you realize, Boj? Your story shows that it is faith in God that will bring results. Not faith in anyone or anything else. Not faith in this country's dream that money and power are the goals that give a person's life all the meaning it needs. Tell your story, Boj. And give your God the glory for it."

"I don't think nuclear warheads give God much glory," Boj snapped, "and they will give him even less if they are ever launched."

"If you do not see the hand of God in all of this, you are lost," moaned a woman.

"If Satan has a hand in this and I cannot recognize it, I am truly lost," whispered Boj.

"Boj!" pleaded a friend who was like a brother to him. "Listen to me. Where are you and where is God? Do you feel close to him?"

"No."

"Is it easy to worship him?"

"No."

"Is it easy to pray to him?"

"No."

"Boj! You are cut off from him! Until you praise him for what he's done you will never get near God. Can't you see that? You're worshipping your idea of God, not God himself. Throw away your obstinacy and see God as he really is."

"I do see him. I must. Have I loved evil? Have I danced with darkness? Have I worshipped Hell?"

"You do not see him. You cannot. You have only loved your own imagination. You are lost!"

Boj's mind burned and swirled with sparks. He could not sleep. He could not eat. What little was left of his praying ceased. The dancing stopped. He did not want to dress in the mornings and he did not want to undress at night. He sat slumped at his desk, draining cups of coffee, the skin of his face sagging from his skull.

Why not? he thought finally. God was God. Could something like this happen without his consent? Maybe he wanted Boj to be rich. Others who loved God were rich. Why not just praise God publicly for it? God had withdrawn himself from Boj. Maybe the lack of gratitude was the reason after all. How could so many others be wrong and Boj right?

He scrubbed his face with both hands so that his flesh reddened. He picked up the receiver of his phone. He would call a public meeting, a press conference. Let everyone come and hear him. They would all be happy. He could have his friends back again. He could sleep. Maybe he could even worship. He punched in the amber button and spoke with his secretary.

The hall downtown was crammed the next morning. The church leaders and dignitaries were pretty sure they knew what was about to occur and most were genuinely grateful, a few were smug.

"God's brought him around," someone affirmed. "This announcement will open the eyes of a lot of people in this country."

Boj stepped from a side door and stood before a battery of microphones. Spontaneously, people began to applaud. Camera flashes flickered over his face like sheet lightning. As he waited for the applause to die down so that he could be heard, he watched the flashes burst all over the hall, tinging smiling faces blue and white. Suddenly the thought pounced upon him like a cougar: These are missile blasts.

In all that Boj had been through, he had never raised his voice at God. He had never permitted anger. He had never shaken his fist, never shouted, never demanded that God explain himself. Now the flashes and the blue-singed skin and all the weeks of pain and frustration rose in him like a ball of hot lava. He flung out his arms and glared over the heads of the people.

39

"My God! Why have you abandoned me? Why have you struck me this blow? Am I your enemy? Am I someone who hates and despises you? I am your friend! Is this how you treat your friends? I have done nothing wrong! How have I abused you? How have I insulted you? I love you! But you have thrown me into the street, you have covered me in filth, you have let men and women cut me to pieces and trample me.

"You have weighed my hands down with war and murder. You have buried me alive in gold. Now you stand back and join those that accuse me. How could you do this? How could you hurl me into the grave? How could you turn your back on my love and my devotion? How could you reject me? Speak to me! Where are you? Turn and face me! I want out! Do you hear me? I want to be free of all this! Am I nobody to you? In God's name, speak!"

By the time Boj had finished his ranting and raving at the ceiling, face purple and swollen as a grape, the hall was swiftly draining of people. "He's gone bonkers!" one minister had shouted. Even the reporters, most of whom were atheists, had taken only a few final photographs before fleeing, glancing nervously at the ceiling as if they expected a thunderbolt from Zeus.

Boj unclenched his fists and hung his head, heart hammering, sweat shining on his scalp. He scarcely heard the words, the thumping of the blood through his head was so loud.

"It's about time you spoke up."

He lifted his head, surprised. The hall was empty.

Within one month, the munitions conglomerate went bankrupt. Boj was restored to a position of greater financial poverty than before he had received his uncle's inheritance. Those who watched Boj's ruin cried, "Aha! You see?" and spoke openly of how God had punished Boj for his ingratitude. The senior minister, upon seeing Boj's fall from wealth, called for the congregational vote that barred Boj from the little church for life. Several television evangelists used Boj's demise to illustrate sermons on God's judgment.

Not only did Boj have to move from his plush neighbourhood, but he had to seek employment at a small school in an obscure rural community—the school board would not allow him to return to his former teaching post. The only room he could afford to rent in that minute community was on the top floor of a large farmhouse which, among other things, boasted nine children under the age of twelve and a huge widow, their mother.

Long after the children were put to bed, the widow would be sitting up in her chair reading a book and three times out of four, she would hear the soft patter of swiftly moving feet coming from the ceiling over her head. She knew her odd, quiet little boarder was dancing up a storm in his room and that was all right with her. She never heard any music though, and that was strange, yet not a cause for great concern. In fact, there was something else.

Didn't she often see the aurora borealis skipping about outside her windows on such nights, even in the dead of summer, and didn't she frequently sense that the air was charged, that there was something in and around her house, a powerful presence? This was odd indeed, yet she had to confess she was never frightened, but instead strangely comforted. She would listen to the rhythm of her boarder's feet until she fell asleep in her chair, book open, and dawn just coming up over the meadow to splash a pail of cold red over the bottom of the sky. She would sleep, and sleep well, while over her head a happy God laughed and panted and danced a hora with his friend.

6

Saint Clancy's Passion

Clancy Lonerhagen liked hamburgers, cop shows, short church services, stockbroking, and women. And he liked God too. God was okay. He'd grown up with God at Sunday School. Clancy attended church, glad when the sermon made him feel good, impatient when the preacher attempted to get under his skin. Sometimes he took his lady friends to church or on outings with his church's singles group. If these women wanted to hang onto Clancy for awhile—he was not an unattractive young man—they learned to like hamburgers, 4X4s, waterskiing, beach parties, and movies where the hero pulled out a huge handgun at the slightest provocation. And God. They had to like God. Clancy didn't drink, he didn't smoke, he didn't swear—he wanted to be on good terms with God at all times.

Clancy loved his country, believed what the newspapers told him, avoided current affairs programs when he turned on his TV. He found it tedious when the minister ranted about justice for the oppressed from the pulpit. Fortunately, Clancy could usually predict when these sermons would occur and on those particular Sundays he would visit his parents across town and attend their own church with them.

Take Pentecost for instance. It was a safe bet that the sermon topic at Pentecost would be on justice and peace. He did have a hard time figuring out on which Sunday Pentecost would fall each year. He knew it was so many weeks after Easter but it seemed to him the choice of the exact Sunday was arbitrary. It was normally announced in the church bulletin the Sunday before however, a convenience for which Clancy was grateful to God. Windy sermons about corrupt governments and unjust laws! It stood to reason that people got what they were asking for if they broke the law with some sort of protest or sign waving or whatever. Clancy kept the law himself, though he did speed a bit on the multi-lane freeway if he was late for church or anxious to get up to the lake on a hot Friday afternoon.

Clancy was waxing his red jeep one Saturday evening when he remembered the next day was Pentecost Sunday. He called up his parents and joined them at their church and for lunch the next day. The following Sunday he returned to his own church and settled into his corner of a pew at the back of the sanctuary. He glanced around to see if Cheryl or Wendy or Nicole were there somewhere, prayed a moment, then opened the bulletin the usher had given him. To his horror the words PENTECOST SUNDAY were printed in bold letters across the top.

It had to be a mistake. It was an old bulletin. He checked the date. The date was right. What had he done wrong? He had to get out somehow, say that he had left something in his jeep, his Bible, his offering envelope. He got up. At that moment, Nicole appeared.

"Clancy," she smiled, "do you mind if I sit with you?"

"Well," said Clancy, "I've just got to get—"

But the organ roared, the choir filed in, the minister boomed his welcome, and the first hymn was being sung before Clancy could move or finish his sentence. He sat down. He would have to tough it out somehow, maybe use the sermon time to work out his plans for Sunday afternoon and evening. After all, here was Nicole, and he could always ask Nicole to join him.

Midway through the service he became dimly aware that another person was sitting at the front of the church beside the minister, but this person was pretty well hidden behind the large oak pulpit. When it came time for the sermon and Clancy began to read the announcments in the bulletin, he was surprised to discover that the person was a Ms. Pieta Zaragoza who was going to speak about the work of God in her country. Clancy's interest was stirred. What did she look like? How long was she staying in town? The minister introduced her and she stood up.

She was stunning. Her short and slender body was wrapped in a navy blue dress. Her hair was long and black and her skin was a rich brown. Her words were clear, her sentences short. Clancy enjoyed her accent, it added to her feminine mystique. She spoke about poverty in her country, and the suspension of habeas something, but she lost Clancy half-way through her talk because he was desperately trying to figure out a way to get free of Nicole and meet Pieta. He wanted to ask her out to dinner that night.

What he did was to excuse himself as soon as she was finished, go out the church's front doors, and sit across the street at a fast food bar gobbling a double cheeseburger. He watched the people streaming out of the church at the end of the service, shaking hands with the minister and with Pieta. When almost everyone was gone, and there were only small knots of people talking on the sidewalk and on the church steps, people who didn't know Clancy, he finished his burger and walked back across the street to the church. He fired off a quick prayer.

At that moment, Pieta gracefully disengaged herself from the couple she was speaking with and stepped back inside the church building, perhaps to get her purse or to use the washroom. Clancy raced in after her. He called her name. She turned. Her eyes were on him. She smiled, took his hand. He thanked her for the talk. He had never had much use for such talks, he said, but hers had changed his mind. The church needed to deal with these issues. Would she care to discuss the problems in her country with him? Was she perhaps free for dinner that night?

"Well," she replied, "I am eating with the minister's family and then I am speaking at a small church downtown. Why don't you come and listen to me there? Perhaps afterward I could answer some of your questions."

The church turned out to be a bunch of long-haired Jesus freaks or whatever, sitting on stacking chairs in their blue jeans and khaki jackets. Clancy was noticeably present in his pale blue suit and tie and crew cut. But Pieta smiled towards him as she stood up to speak and he forgot about where he was and listened to her voice.

They did talk afterwards, but only for a minute, because she was supposed to lead a small group session with some of the church leaders. Clancy asked if he could drive her back to the minister's home later. No, thank you, that was not necessary, as the minister himself was coming to pick her up. Clancy wondered if he could talk with her another night, it was really important to him. She smiled a different kind of smile. She was sorry, but she had a full schedule, she was speaking somewhere every day and every night. She had little time to herself. Perhaps he would like to come to some of her other talks? They might be able to help him understand her country better. He took down a list of the places she was going to speak at. She said good night, turned and walked into the room where the church leaders were waiting for her.

Clancy changed all his plans, called off his racquetball games, cancelled his dates with Tara and Jessica and Kelsey, begged off extra hours with his stockbroking firm. He sat in small churches and big churches and in some buildings which weren't churches at all and where he suspected many of the people were not Christians.

Every night he drank in Pieta's voice and her face and he wondered what it would be like to brush out her hair. After each talk he tried to get close to her, she would see him and smile, but always she had something else to do afterwards and always the minister was coming to see her back to the house safely. Finally, Clancy called the minister and begged to be allowed to take Pieta home just one night in order to talk to her about Christ and the Third World. His wish was granted. That night he was there after her talk and after the long discussion she led in one of the church's Sunday School rooms. He waited impatiently until she was saying good night to each person and was stepping out the door.

"Pieta," he said.

She turned to look at him. She grinned. "So," she laughed, "you are my ride?"

It was a warm night and Clancy had the roof of the jeep down. Her hair flowed back over her neck. He asked if she wanted to stop somewhere for some food or ice cream. She said she was very tired. Clancy took his time getting to the minister's house. He prayed and tried once more: Couldn't he treat her somewhere, for breakfast, for lunch, anything? He had so many questions, her talks were raising more and more issues in his mind. She laughed. Her laugh was strong and shining, out of the deepest parts of herself, not simply her throat. All right, she said, on Friday I do not have to be anywhere until noon. We could have a long breakfast together. Yes, of course, responded Clancy. Is there anywhere special you would like to go? Yes, she told him, I would like to eat breakfast at your place. I want to see where you live.

Clancy phoned in sick Friday. He was up at four in the morning getting everything ready: candles, tablecloth, music. He brought his mother over to make crepes, left the crepes warming in the oven, dropped his mother off back at her home, and picked up Pieta.

She was dressed simply in a black blouse and a long embroidered peasant's skirt. Her hair was pulled back and tied with a red scarf. She laughed at all his jokes. Clancy took her up to his apartment. She enjoyed the crepes. Had he cooked them? In a way, yes. She teased him: Did he have a maid? What did he do to afford such a beautiful apartment? Clancy said he was a stockbroker. She nodded and played with her long-stemmed juice glass. Did Clancy want to ask her some of his questions? She would try to answer them. Clancy shrugged. Tell me where you grew up, he said, tell me what it was like.

Her father had been a farmer. She used to ride on the wagon when he took his vegetables in to sell at the markets in the city. They did not always have enough to eat. There was never enough milk. A brother and a sister, her playmates, died. Clancy said he was sorry. She looked at the framed posters on the walls. Her father and mother had died as well. Clancy put down his fork and knife. From starvation? No, she replied, they were shot. What? exclaimed Clancy. What had they done? They had done nothing, Pieta told him, still looking at the walls. Most of the healthy adults in the village were shot. They wanted the land. For what? Clancy asked. To grow crops for the companies in North America, she said. The children were sent to whatever relatives could be found. I was sent to live with my mother's brother. He had become a wealthy man. He paid for me to go to university in the United States. What did you take? asked Clancy. Law, she answered. I am a lawyer in my country now. I am trying to help the farmers. And I am trying to bring some of the killers to justice. Who are these killers? Clancy wanted to know. They are police and soldiers, she said. Not the police and the soldiers, protested Clancy. Why doesn't the government do something? The government does a great deal, she told him. The government hires them and trains them. Clancy had forgotten his dish of fresh fruit: Your government tells them to kill farmers? Not just farmers, she explained. Lots of people. Maybe even stockbrokers. Why? he asked. The government is what it is, she said. Surely there are some people in your government who aren't like this? demanded Clancy. Yes, there are some, she nodded. Once in awhile I am able to convict a few of the murderers because of the help of these men. But Pieta, Clancy asked, isn't this dangerous? It is dangerous, she agreed, but it is what Christ wants me to do. He did dangerous things. The government hated him. It is the same thing. Don't you try and do what Christ wants you to do?

Pieta glanced at her watch. "I need to get back to the minister's house and change before my talk," she said. "All right," Clancy responded, "I'll take you there. And I'll get you to your talk." "Oh, that isn't necessary," she argued. "You must get back to your work." "No, Pieta," he said. "I want to do it."

She stared at him. "All right, Clancy."

Clancy changed all his weekend plans, went to every talk she gave, listened. He drove her home at the end of each day, the top of the jeep down, her hair blowing back into the night. Once they parked by a river, looked at the lights in it. She talked about a river she had played in near her village. She had made green boats to sail on it out of huge leaves. Had he heard of such and such a plant? No, he hadn't. These leaves were so large you could eat a meal off of them. Even a hamburger, she laughed. She laid her head back and closed her eyes. He watched her, thought about touching her shoulder or her hair, decided not to. She was not Nicole or Wendy or Kelsey. She was somebody else. She fell asleep. He put his jacket over her and drove her to the minister's house. Before she went in she told him her Sunday afternoon was free. Clancy said that his parents had a cabin by a lake, it was only a couple of hours drive, she could swim. It is not as warm here yet as my country, she grinned. I will probably not swim. But I would like to look at the water.

She spoke at another church on Sunday morning and they left right after the service. She changed into a white skirt and white blouse. The whole drive up to the lake she wanted to listen to the radio. Once they got there she wanted no noise at all, just wished to hear the water against the rocks. There was an old canoe Clancy had never used beause he preferred the family's powerboat. He wrestled it into the water. They both paddled. She was good at it. Where had she learned? Her father had had a boat which she had paddled. He tried to ask her more about her work in her country. No, she said, I do not want to talk about that out here. Near evening, she heard a loon call. Clancy imitated the call.

The loon responded, the high notes trembling off the lake and the boulders and the green pine. Pieta tried to call but she could not do it. She said she thought the loon made the freest sound she had ever heard.

Back at the cabin, they ate sandwiches Clancy had thrown together. Then he lent her his sweatshirt because it had cooled off outside. Did she have another talk? Yes. They drove back from the cabin into the city without talking, without a radio. They went straight to the church service. She stood up in her white blouse and white skirt. Clancy watched her move her small brown hands. He reached for a pew Bible, looked up some of the verses she mentioned. There were cookies and cake and tea after the service. Pieta talked to everyone. Clancy stood in a corner and saw her eyes harden, soften, cast out light.

They stopped at the riverbank on the way to the minister's house. She had put his sweatshirt back on. Clancy, she told him, I am going back tomorrow morning. You are not going to drive me to the airport. No, I hate airports. Clancy, I do not want you to think I spent time with you just because I wanted to have some fun. I like you. I think you are a sincere man who does want to know about my country. He looked at her dark hair, touched it, kissed it, kissed her, her mouth was dry, tasted of cake and bread. Pray for me, she said. I am afraid of going back to my country. I was threatened when I left to come and speak in your city. She put her brown hand into his fingers. His mind was empty. He prayed something, thought a bit, prayed something more. She leaned against his shoulder the last few blocks before the house. A smell of wet grass came to Clancy's nostrils. He kissed her hair again, felt its dark weight, took in her scent. She walked into the house, turned and grinned back at him, showed off his sweatshirt, the name of his university in huge initials across the front. I am keeping it, she said.

Clancy Lonerhagen could not sleep. The next morning, he dragged himself across the floor of the stock exchange, lost his racquetball game at noon, staggered home, collapsed on the couch, dreamed of tall green trees and long muddy rivers, Pieta, dirt on her face, washing her blouses and skirts and scarves on the riverbank. He woke up, ate nothing, struggled through another day at the stock exchange, cancelled a long-standing date with Carla, stood in the shower forty-five minutes with the water streaming off his head and back.

He hoped she would write. How long did it take a letter to come from her country? Two weeks? A month? He prayed for her. Slept poorly.

Stopped cooking meals and lived off hamburgers for a week, two weeks. Sat in church. Some of the minister's words reminded him of her words and her words began to sound like Christ's words, the words in red that he looked over in the Bible his mother had given him when he was ten. He kept it open on the kitchen table next to four old pizza boxes. He read it randomly, flipping from here to there. He stood on his balcony one night, half-trying to reach her with his thoughts, asking the Holy Spirit to do it, to tell her how he was feeling, what was going on in his head. There was no moon and the city rose up around him with its squares of light. He remained there until two in the morning, listening to sirens and car tires, facing towards her country, facing her, her hair flowing back like a night.

The stock exchange was quieter the next day. He had two good games of racquetball, won both, came into his apartment whistling. He put on the TV while he stripped for a shower, watching the coloured images, the faces jumping on and off, listened to a report about a famous baseball player charged for possession of cocaine, looked at the anchorwoman reading the news, saw a map of a country, saw Pieta's face come on the screen, saw an ambulance being loaded, a curb spattered with blood, a street full of running people, recent guest in our city, activist, lawyer, law courts, murdered, machine gun, police investigating, sports after this, toothpaste, beer, amazing blow-out sale, THE WORLD'S GREATEST CHOCOLATE BAR!

Clancy stood the same way he had stood when he first stepped in front of the TV to listen to the story about the baseball player. Then he walked a few fet across the carpet, sat down on the floor slowly, curled himself into a ball. After a few moments, the TV shouting weather and sports, he began to weep.

He showed up at the stock exchange in the morning unshaved, his shirt unbuttoned, his body unwashed. Persons ran in front of him, behind him, around him.

"Big day, Clancy!" yelled a man as he raced past. "Most buying I've seen in months. Where the heck have you been?"

Clancy Lonerhagen stood in the middle of the roar, one motionless body. Finally, he began to walk. He found his boss, told him he was quitting, left, wandered up and down city blocks, somehow found the riverbank. Squatted in the mud and grass in his dress pants. The sun hurtled up and over his head, fell down.

He spoke to God, cold, the grass cuts on his palms stinging. It seemed to him that God waited until it was utterly dark before answering. At first, Clancy was not sure who the voice belonged to, it sounded strange, he had not heard it before. They talked all night, Clancy sometimes shouting, sometimes whispering, sometimes getting up and striding back and forth along the bank.

Dawn was the colour of mud. He ran his hands through his crew cut, heard the river, tore the shirt off his back and bent, splashing cold water over his arms and chest and face. Then he straightened, shook his head so that drops of water sprayed around him in the light, and laughed, laughed freely with all his being, laughed with the fire and light of Heaven, just as Pieta had laughed on earth and laughed still.

7

Two Ministers

Once upon a time there were two men who went to seminary to-gether. One of them won high praise from his professors and peers. He was a straight A student. He had his theology down pat. His ora-torical powers were smooth and flawless. His skills in administration were unequalled when he was sent out on pastoral field work. All agreed he would become a model minister. And indeed, any church he pastored grew by leaps and bounds. There was no subject he could not preach on masterfully, there was no question he did not have all the answers for. People flocked to hear his powerful preaching, to experience his energetic and charismatic leadership. Soon he became so popular he was constantly away from his own church, preaching and teaching throughout the country. The people were sorry to have him away so much, but they shrugged their shoulders and accepted that he was God's man for the hour. The only thing they regretted was they could never get close to him. He was too busy and his flawlessness made him too impersonal. If you did manage to arrange for a counselling session with him, he could scarcely empathize with you in your personal strug-gle or sorrow because everything was perfect in his mind and in his life. The cool way in which he counselled you, giving solution after solution to every problem, reminded some of a well-functioning ma-chine. But, his people reasoned, he was a great man, and that was part of being a great man. So they swallowed their hurts and basked in his oratorical power, his theological acumen, his dynamic leadership, and his widespread reputation as a man of God's Word. In church, under the spell of his voice, all became well inside anyway. It was only at home, away from his voice, that the hurts smarted again.

The other of the two men went to seminary the same time as the first man. But they had little in common. This other man was not a straight A student. He fidgeted too much when he was speaking in public and sometimes stuttered. He had a hard time organizing things. He often left questions unanswered on theological examinations, claiming he could discover no one solution to the dilemma of trying to discern what God thought about things God had never spoken about. The seminary did not think he would do well in the ministry and shunted him off to a small pastorate in the backwoods. The congregation did not grow in size. His preaching was quiet and he did not have a lot of solid theological answers when it came to group Bible studies. People complained they had to go home and think about what the answers might be. The man was not charismatic, did not attract a lot of attention at church socials or inter-church events or denominational conventions. But his people shrugged and smiled. Their pastor was not perfect, but they loved him because he loved them. No matter who came to him, or when, he had time for them, and a listening ear for them, and empathy for them. He did not have a lot of answers for those who came to him in pain and dismay, but he had faith and compassion and he gave them hope. They all reflected on how little they thought of him during the week, or after a counselling session, but rather how much they thought of God. It was as if God leaked out of all the seams in their minister's professional ability and theological erudition. How easy it was to get close to him, yet close to God at the same time.

During the course of the two men's lives, the two men did not see much of each other. The first man had no time for the disorganized, inefficient, stuttering little pastor the second man became. He ridiculed him before others and often considered that the man was not a strong Christian because his theology was so unstructured. He could not understand why his congregation did not send him packing. As the first man became more and more famous, the stuttering pastor became less and less of an entity to him, except that the first man often caricatured the second man's personality in his sermons, to illustrate the type of godless and unscriptural minister the age had produced, to the Church's shame.

Finally, the two ministers died and came into the prese55nce of God. The first man was smiling and confident and stood without fear before his Maker. The second man was quiet and sober and knelt with his head down before his God. But when God turned to the first man, God's voice and words shattered the man's flawless composure and drove the smile from his face. God said to him, "Get out of my sight. All your precise theology and precise prayers have made a horrible racket before me. Not a bit of it was done with love or compassion. Your whole life was a blasphemy. Leave my presence at once."

The first man collapsed in fear at these words and lay weeping. God turned to the second man. "But I say to you, well done. Stay with me. Your love for God and people has been my joy and crown." But the second man looked up at God and said, "I cannot stay and remain with you unless I bring this hurting brother with me." God replied, "If you shall accept him, I also will accept him."

The second man turned and looked at the first man and said in a strong voice: "I do accept him." And God looked at the first man and smiled, saying, "Join us and remain in the love and presence of your God."

The first man stared up at the second man in both thankfulness and shame. To his surprise, the man seemed to change before his eyes. In that moment, he saw that the second man was the Christ.

8

Cruciform

He started looking for God when he was two years old. An adult bent near him in the Toddlers' Room at church and showed him pictures and talked about God, but God was not in the pictures. Aaron Fitzgerald kept looking. As he grew up, he looked for God, on various occasions, in his closet, by a stream he caught frogs at, and in a corner of the ceiling at church when the minister stood up and preached in a loud voice. God was not to be found in any of these places and at fourteen Aaron Fitzgerald decided there must not be a God, so he cheerfully joined his friends in shoplifting. They were eventually caught with a great deal of merchandise and the department store chose to prosecute. At sixteen, Aaron went to a minimum security institution designed specifically for young offenders.

One Sunday a minister with a collar came to speak with him and an old interest in finding God sparked him to ask the man a lot of questions. He looked at the minister and he listened to the answers very carefully. He was not satisfied. He neither saw God nor heard God in the man's words. He insisted that the minister not visit him again.

Eighteen found him back in his parents' house and back at his old school. He got together on weekends with the friends he had made in jail. One Friday night they stole a car, drove it while they were drunk, and ran over an old woman and her granddaughter. This time Aaron went to prison.

Prison frightened him. He walked in circles around the yard, men with rifles and machine guns standing above him and watching. Sometimes he would stare up at the brilliantly blue sky and cry out for God without moving his lips. But nothing happened. His parents would visit him, give him colourful tracts. He scanned them, saw nothing, threw them out, grew more and more bitter.

As soon as he was released from prison, he realized that he hated the cities, hated the people who walked around in them, hated the whole world into which he could no longer fit. He decided to get out, to put his hands on enough money and simply disappear. In six months' time, he and four others had arranged the perfect robbery. They carried guns they were confident they would never have to use. But when they blocked off an armoured car on a side street, the guards came out shooting. Aaron and the four others fired back. They killed every guard. But the police arrived before they could escape.

The five of them were sentenced to death, but each of them had their sentence commuted to life imprisonment except Aaron Fitzgerald. He had planned the robbery, opened fire at the guards first and incited the others, and had never shown a trace of remorse over the killings. A chaplain came to visit him on death row but Aaron was a long way past seeing anything now. He told the chaplain to get out.

They came for him a few hours before midnight in the middle of April. They placed him in a room, sat him in a chair, shaved a patch of hair from the back of his head, shaved a couple of inches on each leg and both arms, attached wires. He was minutes from death. He was afraid. He gazed down at those sitting to witness his execution and he cursed them as loudly as he could.

A guard tightened the leather straps over his ankles and wrists, cinched them so fiercely his circulation was cut off and pain ripped up his arms. It subsided to an aching throb as the nails were hammered flush with his skin, then tore through his body with a ferocious force as he was lifted up on the cross and the cross was dropped clumsily into a deep hole. He had never experienced this intensity of pain before and he screamed.

Flies buzzed in and out of his mouth, the sun raked his face and chest, blood ran out of his hands and feet and out of his nose onto his chin and stomach. He was thirsty, his tongue was swollen, he could hardly get a breath because the weight of his entire body seemed to be crushing down on his lungs. He choked, he vomited, he gulped and gurgled for one more mouthful of air. He looked at the man dying on the cross next to him, a man obviously cut by whips, whose face was barred with lines of blood that had worked their way down from his lacerated forehead and scalp, a man sweating and struggling and gasping for breath just as he was, and looking at him Aaron saw. It was not the kind of situation in which he would have expected to find God. It was the last place he would have looked.

9

The Las Vegas God

At first, all goes well.

He marries an outstanding woman, he invests money wisely, he becomes a millionaire. He makes international news early on when he hands Mother Theresa a cheque for for fifty million dollars. "My tithe," he laughs.

All the Christian talk shows want to interview him. "God made me rich," he tells them. "I give the good Lord the credit. There are certain universal laws that God has laid down. Provided you go along with them and don't commit any violations, God will bless you. It's as sure as gravity. And we're not just talking about spiritual blessings, as important as those are, of course. We're talking about the material world. The Lord knows we need money. He used money when he was on the Earth. He had flesh and bones to feed. He had to put clothes on his back. He needed money. So he gives us money too. My favourite Bible verse is that one where Paul says, 'My God will supply all your needs according to his riches in glory.' Yes, amen. My own life proves the truth of that. I made my first million selling pews to churches. Now that's a fact."

James Oscar Buttering; his face on *Time*, *Newsweek*, and *Christianity Today*. A model home. A model wife. A model car. All postpaid from God.

He played God the way some men play VLTs or the machines at a casino. He reasoned that if he pumped in enough prayers, enough worship services, enough charity and tithe money, sooner or later God would come across with paydirt—the right business merger when Buttering needed it, the right car, the right solution for a critical family problem. He was not an insincere man. He considered that his tithing and his church attendance and his humanitarian deeds were investing in God—he expected a return on his investment. And God always came through. He was not only practical with his blessings but dependable. You might even say predictable. You live holy and give God ten percent of your income and don't swear or smoke and sure as the sun would rise God would fix you up like the Prince or Princess of Wales on their wedding day. He had another favourite Bible verse, "Come unto me all you that labour and are heavy-laden and I will give you rest," but he always misquoted it, saying instead, quite innocently, "Come unto me all you that labour and are heavy-laden and I will give you the rest."

But troubles will attend even the most rock-solid investment. And after you've lived a while you know, as William Shakespeare said, that troubles prefer to travel in bunches, they like to keep each other company. So it was for James Oscar Buttering.

First it was his wife. She left to find herself. Then it was his home: half his children wound up on drugs and the other half disappeared. Then it was his car, or at least one of his cars—it broke down, utterly fell apart, on his way to work. When he finally got another limousine out to where he was stranded on a traffic-jammed freeway, it was only to pick up his car phone and learn that oil prices had plunged, ruining a third of all his investments. But not to worry. Diversification. Unfortunately, the troubles had learned all about diversification themselves.

A revolution the government had sworn to him would never get off the ground did, destroying his coffee stocks. His airline went bankrupt. South Africa froze his diamond assets. His fleet of luxury liners all went down in the same harbour on the same day due to a freak out-of-season storm. He couldn't collect on the insurance because none of his vessels was carrying coverage for that kind of storm. "It wasn't an act of God," said the broker, "it was a typhoon, and as you see, clause F.4 specifically rules out coverage in the event of a typhoon."

By the time James Oscar Buttering got to his office, it was all he could do to push through the reporters, the stock brokers, the government officials, the politicians, the bank managers, and last, but not least, the lawyers, and get into his private washroom to take the rumpled, sweat-stained shirt off his back—the state in which James Oscar Buttering remained the rest of his life. Peeking out behind the wash-room door, he wondered that there wasn't a clergyman or two on hand in the crowd to administer last rites. There wasn't, but they showed up soon enough.

It was a week later and James Oscar Buttering had just finished lining up at the food bank and he had his feet up because they hurt like blazes. He had a cold room in a warehouse with a hot plate and a seaweed green fridge. He had been living on macaroni and Libby's beans for five days and was resting a bit before he got back on his feet and started to boil the macaroni for the required seven minutes. His thumb was bandaged, sliced open on a can of Campbell's chicken noodle soup, a low calorie can, as a matter of fact. James Oscar Buttering still had enough left in him to snicker at someone's concern for the poor's cholestrol intake. He'd forgotten what butter and eggs and red meat looked like and he'd already lost thirteen pounds.

The clergymen, however, three or four of them, had not lost any weight in a long time. In fact, they were quite plump—a sign of grace according to James Oscar Buttering's pre-bankruptcy theology. All of them had known him in his earlier life. Now they sat around on such things as they could find to sit around on. They coughed and smiled and mentioned the weather. Finally, they got to the point: Did James Oscar Buttering want to pray?

"Not particularly," said Buttering.

The clergymen exchanged glances. One of them leaned forward.

"James," he said, "this mess won't straighten itself out until you lay it all before God and ask for forgiveness."

"Me?" snorted Buttering. "Why should I be asking God for forgiveness? God should be asking me."

That started it. The clergymen began to accuse Buttering of arrogance and blasphemy and of having a cold heart towards God. They probed for the sins that had led God to punish him with his bankruptcy. When he answered one, another immediately began to argue with him.

"You have said it yourself a thousand times," they cried. "If you are good and holy, God will take care of you and bless you. But if you break God's laws in some way you can expect trouble and a miserable life. Isn't this what has been happening to you?"

"I did nothing wrong!" Buttering raged. "I did no sin. I never shirked any of my responsibilities. I went to church. I tithed. I prayed. And this is how God repays me. He ruins an innocent man. I loved God but where has it gotten me? You think I'm corrupt, my former business colleagues sneer at me when I shuffle by in the streets, people look the other way when they see me sitting in the park, even children call me names and throw things at me. This is how God rewards his friends. I shouldn't have wasted my time being so good and religious."

"Ungrateful man!" the clergymen responded. "After all God has done for you!"

"God was just playing with me the way a cat plays with a bird," snarled Buttering. "He was setting me up for the fall. Now I'm here, right where he wants me. God betrayed me!"

Buttering made a fist and raised it towards heaven, shaking it, his face clenched in anger.

"Who do you think you are?" roared Buttering. "Who do you think you are?"

Prayer can be an interesting thing, for certainly, shouted as it may have been at the top of his lungs, what Buttering had uttered had still been a prayer. We often pray because we were raised by our parents to pray, or because the Bible and the minister say we ought, or because it makes us feel good inside, or because we're desperate. Whatever prayer means or doesn't mean to us, we certainly would be surprised to realize God was actually listening, God, the Maker of the worlds, the Spirit beyond time and beyond earth. Imagine if God talked back. There we are, mumbling something over our chicken and salad, and a voice comes back at us out of thin air.

In this respect, James Oscar Buttering was very little different from any of us. Prayer was fine, but there was work to do, and even Jesus had said he had to be about his Father's "business." So James Oscar Buttering had prayed dutifully and worked heartily and when he raised his fist to God and raged it was, if not exactly rhetorical, certainly a personal indulgence, a venting of his emotions. He did not expect an answer. He got one.

It is difficult to relate exactly what happened.

Talking to the clergy about it later, they merely glanced away and muttered a few indistinct phrases. James Oscar Buttering would nod and sometimes smile and say things like: "I looked into my soul." Or even worse: "I looked into God's soul."

Apparently, what had occurred was this: As James Oscar Buttering shook his fist at the sky, or to be precise in this instance, the warehouse ceiling, a voice came crashing out of the rafters, "I am not a Las Vegas slot machine, James Oscar Buttering." Then, instead of the usual Hollywood pyrotechnics, a breeze fresh with the smell of earth, and forest in the rain, and salt sea blew through the warehouse. Nor was the voice a bass.

What God said in that warehouse full of wonderful breezes and scents went something like this: "I'm not your good luck charm. I do not fit into your wallet with your credit cards. I am not a bank. You do not find me in toy stores. You do not find me in pet stores. You cannot put a leash on me. I do not do tricks. I am not for sale. I am not a Pisces or a Capricorn or an Aquarius. You cannot predict me. I am not your employee. You cannot hire me. I do not answer to your laws. I do not answer to you. I am, James Oscar Buttering, the living God, and you are not my equal."

When I was piecing all this together, I looked Buttering up. He was hoeing a modest squash patch behind his small home. He had remarried and his children, one still struggling with an addiction, lived with him and his new wife. It had been an extremely warm fall and a thunderstorm was coming on. It was that still and calm half-hour before it broke that we talked, he leaning on his hoe, I leaning against the white picket fence.

"I'll tell you what came out of it," he said. "We hear a lot about wife abuse and child abuse these days. We even hear about animal abuse. But we never hear about God abuse. I was using God. I couldn't take him as he was. I could only have a relationship with him if he was the kind of God I would be if I was God. He had to measure up to my standards. He had to be my "yes" man. Or he wasn't worth having. I've learned since then to get to know him. I've learned to value him for who he is, not for what I can get out of him."

Buttering died a few years later of leukemia. The pain was intense. I visited him once in hospital and his face was shrivelled and far away. He was muttering under his breath. Then he looked up at me. "I am angry about this disease," he whispered. "At the warehouse God told me he had answered me because it was the first time I'd been honest with him. He said he could handle criticism and he told me to keep it up. I have."

I was the only one at the cremation. His new wife had lost interest in him when he had contracted his illness and his children were living their own lives in other parts of the country. I kept the urn and buried it in my garden to see what would grow over it. But I kept a handful of ashes in my pocket and climbed a hill near my home. I threw the ashes into the air and the wind snatched them, sifted them, and carried only a few of them off. It seemed appropriate.

10

The Bible Study

N ow there were two women. Both went to different churches but they got together once a week to talk with each other and to discuss the things of God. The first woman was in a Bible study group that helped them learn what they were supposed to believe. They merely directed their questions to the leader of the Bible study, a pastor, and he gave every question a definite answer. They simply had to memorize what he told them and they had the solution to each of their problems. This brought them great satisfaction and a great deal of peace.

The second woman attended a Bible study in her church where the leader, also a pastor, would not give them definite answers to their questions. In fact, he hardly gave them any answers at all, but instead preferred to answer their questions with another question, which would get them thinking about why they had asked their questions in the first place. They wound up reading the Bible on their own, even praying, and they always came back to the Bible study group with more complex questions than the simple ones they'd started out with. This did not bring a great deal of peace, it brought about a great struggle within each person. Some of the members of this Bible study group left—they wanted a Bible study where they would be able to get plain yes and no answers to their questions, plus whatever additional information the pastoral leader might deem appropriate. After all, why were they paying this fellow?

Despite all this, the second woman enjoyed the Bible study, enjoyed the struggle, though it sometimes cost her sleep, though it sometimes cost her peace of mind and heart.

When the two women got together, the first woman would say: "How good our Bible study leader is, how wise, how many answers he has, he has set everything straight for me. I have the understanding I craved for all the things that happen in my life. I have found peace and truth."

And the second woman would say: "I cannot tell you that I have answers for all the things that happen in my life. I cannot say I have peace or have all the truth. But I certainly have prayed more and read the Scriptures more since I joined this Bible study group. I feel I am wrestling with God."

"Well," responded the first woman, "suit yourself, but if you ask me, anyone who lacks peace in their Christian life isn't getting enough of the teaching they need."

So the one woman had her peace and the other woman had her struggle.

It happened that in the first woman's church, her Bible study leader, the pastor, had an affair with another woman in the study group. It was discovered and he was fired from the church. Soon after, the first woman experienced a suicide in her family, and then her husband contracted cancer, followed by her youngest child being diagnosed with multiple sclerosis. These blows, falling one after another, shattered her peace, and when she sought answers from the Scriptures, she could not find them. The answers the disgraced pastor had given her, all of which she'd memorized, seemed empty. She did not know who to turn to and there was little within her own self to rely upon, her faith had been built on her pastor's, and her pastor's faith had fallen. He was living with the woman he'd had the affair with. He told anyone that tried to contact him that he was sick of performing and of having to play God. He wanted nothing more to do with churches or Christians. The first woman was crushed.

The second woman also experienced a good deal of hardship at this time. Her husband was pinned under a heavy piece of metal at work. One leg was severed at the knee. He was bitter and angry. The woman's children could not accept their father in this state, nor could they talk to him, so they stayed out increasingly, kept away from the house. She agonized about the trouble they might get into. On top of it all, her mother, with whom she was very close and in whom she confided everything, suddenly collapsed with a stroke. By the time the woman had made it to the hospital her mother had lapsed into a coma. She did not know where to turn—except to where the struggles of the Bible study had always taken her. She fell on her bed and prayed to God and poured out the pain of her heart.

Catching her by surprise, many truths she had fought and struggled with God over welled up in her to answer her cries. She knew them to be real for she had wrestled them through for herself. This was no second-hand faith God had fashioned in her. The Scriptures blazed with light. No, it was an authentic faith God had personally forged in her soul. She was able to get up off the bed with the peace she had never had before. When she learned of the plight of her friend, she went to her immediately and gave her the strong comfort she could out of the peace and faith God had worked in her own heart. And together, through the Word, through prayer, through the Spirit, and through the fire, the two women entered into life—a new and hitherto undreamed of reality between themselves and the One who was there for them.

11

The Far Kingdoms
of the Blue Night

I was born when my father was 38, the first child. He did not become more cautious because he had a son to provide for. Within a few months of my birth he decided he must finally begin to ski down the slopes of mountains. He also was determined to climb them with rope and ice axe and crampons biting into snow and rock. He went hunting, not to kill—he never did shoot anything—but to draw as close to the animals as he dared, to cougar and moose and grizzly. He wanted to do everything that he had imagined himself doing but had never done because the risk intimidated him. Mother told me it was as if one life concluded at my birth and another began minutes after I began to cry and my flesh began to brighten with red and pink. She said it was because he wanted to be a young father for me, someone who could keep up with the other fathers in their twenties. He wanted me to be proud of him, wanted me to see him strong and full of new mornings.

"That's not all of it," he told me when I was twelve. "Yes, I do want to be young for you, not some fat wheezing parson who can only cheer you on from the sidelines. But I want to live a few more lives with you too. Why did we wait until I was 38 to have you?"

I shrugged. We were sitting in a nature park by our home, leaves like cornflakes all around us, and our two dogs yipping and leaping up a pine tree after a squirrel.

"I was afraid of your mother dying in childbirth. Then I was afraid of you growing up and getting into drugs or into a gang or hating me or hating God because I was a minister. I loved the mountains, always hiked in them. I wanted to press my heart against them and let it beat into the stone but I was afraid of getting that close. What if I fell? I wanted snow from my skis to burn my face and melt like a rainfall. I wanted to slash down through the pines and all the cold whiteness. What if I fell? So I stayed at a distance from all the magnificence. You were born. I wanted us to go into the splendour together. I had to try. There were too many fears. I had to plunge into them like a mountain river, feel all the fire and the cold and the sting, and climb up on the other bank, having got somewhere. I'm talking too much. Do you know what I'm trying to get across?"

I did not know then. It bothered me when he used so many words so quickly like that, as if he were speaking faster and faster and might fall apart.

"Forget it," he said. "Let's go see Mom."

Then he was silent and sure and strong, walking back with me through the forest, yes, and into the mountains, onto the slopes, pitching in the great sea in a small kayak, building a fire with no match in wilderness where we knew no one could protect us. I did not know what he meant about facing fears. What did my father fear? Surely he had always been like that, always skiing and climbing and hunting deep into the manless earth. He could use his body as well as anyone. And when words came from him, they came many times like shooting stars blistering a constellation.

To earn a living he preached and counselled and led people—he hoped—into the presence of God. And he wrote stories and published them and the money fed us and clothed us and sometimes mother nursed at the hospital and the moon was full and the world turned round and round. He did not have to worry about us running from him or mother or their God. Why would you hate a God my father compared to a pond, or to a cataract, or a massive cornice of snow and flickering ice? Who would flee a God who fashioned eagles and fox kittens and the far kingdoms of blue night? There was no fear.

We lived, my brothers and sisters and I, and grew up on an island in the North Pacific where there was an infinity of shores and where we could watch the seashells crackle into sand. There were huge waves that thumped like a thudding heart under your feet and mountains bristling with lion and bear and roaring with glaciers and their rapids. Yet my father always looked restlessly over the sea to the mountain range you could spot on the mainland, white peaks that floated above the waters like the high towers of a fantasy.

"Out past those are the real mountains of the earth," he would say. "The Himalayas are beautiful, as heavenly as the white stars. But the Rocky Mountains are the true stuff of earth, rugged and solid and crammed with light, impossible to ignore. Somehow they are rooted in the centre of everything that matters, they are fastened to God. We have to go to them."

We always did go to them. Camping in southern Alberta. Riding horses in the foothills west of Calgary. Wandering along the Bow River near Canmore looking for flat stones. Standing in our skis on the razor peaks scattered about Lake Louise. Yet he seemed most excited when he could draw us into the mountains and long fields of Banff.

He ignored the fact that Banff was a tourist town and he never considered himself a tourist. He enjoyed the bookstore, mother the shops and restaurants, we often hiked up past the graveyard to the School of Fine Arts at the Banff Centre to listen to musicians or to watch the plays. But it was really those tall grey monoliths he came for and, sparkling at their feet, the red deer.

He swore the elk would sense his true intentions and allow him to come close. He was not reckless but he felt the animals would understand him and not run. Mother would get upset because this was the same way he acted in grizzly or cougar country, hoping one would pop up at his elbow and begin to converse with him about the vagueries of heaven and earth.

One year the elk were particularly numerous in Banff and he was anxious that he and I walk out from the Banff Springs Hotel towards the forest and have a long day's communion with the huge beasts. But I was a sophsticated thirteen-year-old and would not go.

"Animals don't talk, Dad," I said. Period.

"Of course they talk. Let's go. The others can swim in the pool."

I wanted to swim in the pool. "They're just animals."

"No animal is just an animal. It will only take an hour. Soon you'll be in university and long gone."

From the time I was ten he constantly informed me I was going to be in university soon. I put on my jacket and followed him past the outdoor pool and the steam rising from its surface. One of my brothers hooted at me and splashed. I decided to enjoy being the eldest, the one privileged to go on dangerous adventures with Dad, and I merely showed my brother my back. We followed a path down to the Spray River, then crossed a bridge and walked through a spattering of spruce trees. I was slouching, no longer needing to put on a show for my brothers and sisters, wishing I could be with them in the pool or banging away on the spangled video games in the hotel's arcade. Father had stopped and I looked past him.

An elk herd was grazing on a field surrounded by trees on three sides. The field was actually one of the hotel's fairways but it was autumn and the course was closed. One of the elk had a large rack of antlers that swung like a pair of swords whenever he glanced up and swivelled his head and neck. There were fifteen elk cropping grass. Even though it was November no snow had fallen. Their breath was like white smudge marks in front of their nostrils.

We were about one hundred and fifty yards away. Father wanted to get closer. He knew elk had charged persons who came too close but he was in a mood. God would reach out and touch us somehow through the animals. So we crept nearer. A few of the females began to squeak back and forth, like seals by the Pacific.

"What do you think they're saying?" father asked me.

I was still sulky. "They're not saying anything."

"Of course they are. They're probably talking about us."

His eyes were rippling with light, the sun leaping in and out of balls of cloud over our heads. He decided we should not get any closer just then but go farther on and follow a trail into the woods. It was littered with elk pellets and mud churned up by large hooves. A musky scent lay over the trees and bushes. I scrunched my shoulders against a sudden feeling clattering up my back.

"Dad, let's go back."

"Why?"

"We should go back. The elk are too big."

"You don't have to be afraid. The elk will sense our intentions."

"What if they don't?"

"They will. I want you to think that way."

Two shapes suddenly appeared ahead of us on the trail. They were large and moving at a slow trot towards us. Father stopped.

"We'll head back," he said.

I turned and began to stride, my long legs carrying me at a lope.

"It's all right," father called, "they won't hurt us."

"How do you know?"

We emerged from the trees and struck out across the fairway. The herd did not pay us any attention. I was heading for the bridge over the river. The more distance I put between the elk and myself, the better I felt.

Six elk broke across the river in front of my father and I. They had smelled us and become alarmed, chopping through the shallow water in a thunderclap of spray and gravel. The herd on the fairway lifted their heads. The six elk ran up to them and the herd began to pace back and forth. The two elk from the trail burst out of the woods at a gallop and the herd grunted and began to run towards us and the river.

"Don't move," father ordered. "They'll outrun you to the bridge and go right over you."

My heart twisted and a jolt made my whole body tighten. The elk bore straight down on us. There was a buzzing in my head and I began to experience a sense of detachment, that somehow the elk were not pounding across the grass at us, that I was watching it all from such a great distance I was safe, these were only vivid images. The herd roared past us, balked at the river, then raced back up to the fairway, passing by us on the other side. Their necks were straight up, their noses thrusting, their run became more like fast prancing, but they did not stop. Once they reached the top of the fairway they twisted and hammered towards us again. Father put his arm around my back and shoulder. I could smell them as they banged past, swung on the gravel at the river bank, and pelted alongside us back to the field.

The circle they had created around us became tighter each time they hurtled back at us. I could see the grass splitting under their hooves. My heart cracked at my chest and I opened my mouth. Father's grip was tight. He pulled me to himself. The herd flew around us again and again. Their eyes became larger and larger, like monstrous black marbles. The bull elk jumped out of the swirl and faced us, antlers chopping from side to side. As he confronted us, the herd began to slow, a few stopped, they all stopped, poised, their legs ready to fly again, their heads up, watching us and their master, their profiles strong and dark.

The bull elk reared his head and trumpeted at us, that powerful and frightening call with its staccato climax of gusts and wails, frightening because it seemed to us a scream, because it seemed a pent-up screeching of wildness. Twice more he cried out, stamping a front hoof, snapping his rack in the cool air. Then he ceased.

For several minutes he watched us, standing utterly still, surrounded by his herd. Finally he dropped his head and began to eat. The others began to graze too. The circle became looser, some of the animals drawing closer to us, others moving a bit further away into the field.

After awhile, father said we could sit down. We squatted on the grass. No one paid us any attention. Elk moved past us, practically stepping over us, but we were no longer threatened. Yet we did not feel free to go. Once I jerked my hand because a stone suddenly pricked it and the bull elk glared at me and snorted, throwing up his head. He stared me down, then resumed his eating. But he never moved any distance from us.

"I feel like we're prisoners," I whispered to my father.

He was not smiling. "We can see it that way or we can see it as a privilege. He could have charged us and he didn't."

"I'm afraid, Dad."

"Try to see that they're accepting us."

"But how long do we have to stay here?"

"They'll move on. Bit by bit. They'll spread out."

"I thought you said they could understand our intentions?"

"What makes you think they haven't? How many people are allowed to sit in the ring of a wild elk herd?"

The clouds had disappeared and the sun ran over the mountains, slewing light. The herd gradually broke the ring that had clasped us. A few crossed the river. Others drifted up by the forest to nibble. Two or three grunted and nestled down only a few yards from me. An hour went by. The bull elk finally turned his back on us and stepped carelessly and powerfully up to the far end of the field, at least 200 yards away.

"All right," father said in a quiet voice. "It's time to leave."

We stood slowly. The elk that had bedded down near us merely glanced as we walked carefully past. We reached the bridge, which was a place of safety, a quick passage to the hotel and its high stone walls.

But once I reached the bridge I did not want to go any further. I looked back at the herd and I looked at the bull, his antlers sparring with the sky as he bent to feed.

"Did he talk to us, Dad?" I asked. I no longer felt fear. I knew the bull elk was a mighty animal, but I also felt I had been special to it. I had been close enough to touch it. I had sat in its presence.

Father leaned his hands on the side of the wooden bridge. "I suppose he did talk to us."

"So can you tell me what he said?"

The tip of the sun was fastened to the sharp slant of a mountain.

"You can get close," Dad answered. "Close enough to get over your fear. Close enough to get rewarded. But the awe never leaves. The adrenaline never stops. When you get that close it's always a miracle. You can hear them. They can listen to you. But you can't be them."

We walked up past the pool. My brothers shouted.

"What'd you see?"

"Nothing," I answered.

"Didn't you see any elk?"

"No."

"Didn't you see anything?"

"No."

"You've got to take us to the arcade now. Mom said."

"I'm too old for that stupid stuff."

I did go to the arcade and the video games though. Not just then but later, when my brothers and sisters had to stay in their beds, I went down and thumped furiously on the machines, the lights bursting like firecrackers. I tried to bury the hour in the field, it was too strong, I didn't want to think about it. But later I had words to understand it, rhythms to make sense of it, and father did too, the man who had faced all his fears when his first son was born, and now let his words of Christ flash like stones under fast water, and I alone in the pews understood. I alone heard the truth of God in a running circle of elk, in a slash of curving antlers, in a cry unknowable, yet impossible to misunderstand or refuse love.

12

The Carol Ships

"Yes, Jonathan."

"But why? Look, Spence, I don't care what a few sour apples in your congregations may have said, you're a good pastor."

"Jonathan, at the end of the twentieth century in North America, you're a good pastor only if you choose one of four options: Bend with whatever political wind blows strongest in your church at any given time. Or permit yourself to become deified by your congregation—no, not only permit it, encourage it, publish books, become famous, start a movement, hold seminars across the country. Or become utterly autocratic, dictatorial, surround yourself with an Old Guard and rule the church with an iron fist. Paternalize. Spoon feed everyone. Let them know you're God's anointed. Or choose the final option—abuse them. Churches love to be yelled at, love to feel guilty, because then they think something spiritual is going on."

"Come on, Spence, it's not that bad."

"I swear, it's like any abusive relationship, like the woman who won't leave the wife-battering husband. As long as a pastor tells the congregation they're no good, they don't measure up, they'll continue to hang around. But the pastors that love them, lose them. They don't understand love or grace as a spiritual force. Just guilt. And I'm tired of everyone wanting to feel bad about themselves because that's the only way they can comprehend that God is actually touching their lives."

"If the Church is so dysfunctional then how come it still manages to do so much good?"

"What impact are we having on our culture? Renewal here, we yell. Renewal there, we shout. Nothing changes. No one is saved. We recycle believers from church to church, denomination to denomination. We're a people of God, bored silly. And to amuse ourselves we bait and manipulate pastors and church leaders. We play at spiritual warfare like it's a computer game wrapped up in glitzy CD-ROM packaging. Ordinary day-to-day Christianity, dying to self, laying down our lives for our neighbours, the daily grind of the holy—who needs it? It's much more fun to scan end-time books for clues to the identity of this year's candidate for Anti-Christ, swoon and fall on floors and luxuriate in the thrill of a Disney World God, shoot doctors who perform abortions, holler and bully and threaten at election time, chase the latest movement of God from city to city. Angels and demons and vortexes and spiritual mapping. Is the West any better for it? Have morals changed? Is there less abuse or rape or divorce or murder? It's junk, Jonathan. The Church is a scrap heap at the end of a millenium."

"So you go into law."

"That's right."

"And that system swallows you up too. Talk about godlessness..."

"They never pretended to be holy. We do. Otherwise, I don't see much difference between the church and the legal system. They're both chaotic, both corrupt, both claim to have a handle on the truth but both do a good job of making a mess of that truth. You know what I look forward to? Not having to let my guard down. Protecting myself, legitimately, from the stab in the back. Feeling safe because I'm not required by holy orders to be vulnerable to everybody. Having rules that everyone must play by, or else."

Jonathan got up and ran a hand through his hair. Spencer was pacing. They were in Spencer's church office. Spencer was announcing his resignation to the congregation the next morning, a Sunday.

"Okay, Spence. You love venting. I'm always the straw man. Do what you have to do. Is God with you?"

"Absolutely."

"I suppose you've spoken with Dick?"

"I have. He told me he's found his job as a tour bus operator more fulfilling than anything he experienced as a pastor."

"Great. And what if Moses had gone back to his father-in-law's sheep or Jesus had gone back to his lathe?"

"If I was Moses or Jesus, God would push me harder. He's giving me an out. Jonathan, there's better ways to serve God in the twenty-first century than meeting a corrupt Christianity's expectations for the pastoral ministry."

"I think the faith is losing a superb advocate. Will you ever preach again?"

Spencer shrugged and slumped down into a chair. Jonathan tried to smile but he was drained.

"Okay, Spence. Okay, brother. God bless you. Merry Christmas."

"Jonathan."

"What?"

"I loved them, Jonathan."

Spencer sat in his office as the afternoon grew dark and poured through the windows over his desk and carpet and face. Then he pulled on his overcoat and went into the street. It had stopped raining. Traffic hissed back and forth. Lights rippled over the slick asphalt. He decided to walk down to the waterfront.

He bought some hot chestnuts. Spencer disliked the texture of the warm nuts when he placed them in his mouth but he liked the heat of the bag against his palm. Some people were singing carols, the music drifting to him as if it was somehow in the mist rolling up from the sea. There were sparks on the water. Sliding towards the beaches and the marinas. Spencer recognized the dark mass of a hull, coloured lights burning holes in the grey and black of the December night. The carol ships. He walked closer to the water's edge, his shoes smacking against the wooden boardwalk.

He'd first heard them here when? A divinity student. He snorted. God Almighty, he'd been full of heaven and all the stars then. Believed the people of God wanted all that God wanted for them. Believed they longed to live and breathe the New Testament. He'd heard the ships another time too. After divinity school. A fine winter's night. Clear and sharp and deep as all time. Just before his first church. Full of spiritual and intellectual fire, a thousand doors springing open in his soul and in his mind. Both times he had sung along with the carol ships, fifteen years younger, not caring who listened, singing to God, singing to the ages. He lingered at the waterfront. His anger at feeling betrayed by the very people he'd given his life to serving, an anger it seemed he had to express daily and vehemently, subsided as he listened to the carols. He realized he needed them, as much as he still needed to know God was setting him free. Born that man no more may die. The carols did not accuse him or fill him with regret at leaving a vocation that had been a steady focus since his conversion at thirteen. He felt he had now sepa-rated himself from a kind of Christian Babylon that had suppressed his personality and even his spirituality. The more carols he heard, the more he believed again, the more alive he felt. When the ships moved off into the dark waters, he stood alone in a sort of gentle rapture, as if he had been newly baptized.

He moved his family east for law school. He thought he had men-tally prepared himself for it but the entire experience was harsher, more demanding, more exhausting than he had anticipated. Unlike semi-nary, there were no prayers, no inspirational messages directed to him that were grounded in God. He fought alone. He struggled to attend church with his wife and children but gave up the plan early on of being part of a small group during the week. When his training was completed, he was offered an opportunity to return to the west coast and article with a firm interested in harnessing his developing exper-tise in natural resources and environmental law. After the move back west he begged off church more frequently. His wife quarrelled with him about it three or four times and then it was never brought up again.

Back and forth he strode from house to office, a laptop and cell phone and legal briefs in his black case. Soon they had a house, a wonderful kind of house, something they could never afford when he had been pastoring small churches. They had savings, an extra car, plenty of food. He found he was working just as hard as he had worked as a minister but agonizing less. And he had a sense of being valued at his firm, an experience that had been only fleeting during his fifteen years as a pastor.

One Christmas he was interviewing a client at a restaurant on the waterfront when the carol ships docked nearby, floating on light, voices streaming. His client nodded.

"Bloody beautiful, eh? One time in the year life can make sense."

"Sure," Spencer responded.

Later, in bed, his wife asleep, his children asleep, alone, no moon, no stars, he wondered why he had felt nothing that evening when the carol ships had docked. He sensed an immense, flat, grey sea in him, smooth and featureless as iron. The music and its passion had glanced off. This had never happened before. He scrubbed his face with his hands.

There was a brief, piercing season a few years later. They had been attending a contemporary church that a law partner also attended and, desperately it seemed to him, he embraced everything about it, the drowning man clutching at flotsam: the informality, the brash music, the gifts of the Spirit, people shouting and thrashing as they were being prayed over— he grasped tightly to every bit of it, a zealot. For two years he rarely missed a Sunday service or Wednesday evening small group meeting. People commented that he articulated his faith well. One older woman asked if he had considered leaving law to become a pastor. He was elated. During this period he heard the carol ships again, but again the music flew over him like a flock of pigeons. Only one thought lanced through his mind: "The notes and lyrics are archaic."

In time, Spencer's enthusiasm for the renewal movement faded. He grew tired of the new legalism he saw developing, where certain things had to happen or God was not perceived to be at work, grew tired of those who wanted the Things rather than the God, became weary with the persons who fell in the Spirit so often he believed the experience was sought for its narcotic effect, turned from the increasingly simplistic choruses with their increasingly childish lyrics and predictable melodies. His wife was not sorry to slip away either, sensing as she did the worship of worship and the worship of the dramatic, so she said nothing at his withdrawal. But she continued to pray for a deepness to gleam in his eyes again.

An opportunity presented itself to take a Doctorate in Common Law at Oxford in England. For several years the family lived among the spires and quadrangles and the hurly-burly of the university city. Spencer loved being a student again, worked hard, was glad to be free of the law practice. His children were now twelve and fourteen and he enjoyed spending more time with them. They travelled as a family all over England, Scotland, and Ireland. He managed to avoid boat trips to Iona and Lindisfarne that the rest of the family went on. God was a truism and transcendent and that is where Spencer preferred him to stay. Only once did a shaft cut straight in.

They attended a carol service at Magdalen College as a family on

Christmas Eve the second year. The arrangements were more ornate but he thought of the ships and the light and his youth and a God lively and childlike and spattered with hay and drops of dung in a stable. Abruptly, he put a hand to his forehead and shut his eyes.

"Are you tired, honey?" his wife asked.

"God, yes."

They returned home to the west coast. He was offered a position at a prestigious law school and took it. Soon after he dreamed of himself on a headland in the sea and, detached from the figure with his face, he watched the headland steadily recede, so that the possibility of knowing this person who remained behind, this person who was himself, though desirable in the dream, seemed more and more remote. The children left home. His wife bought a dog that didn't shed. The house suddenly grew more immaculate than it had ever been during the past twenty years. But there was no sound, no sudden gusts of laughter or delight, and no one touched.

The divinity school at the university where he taught law asked him to teach a course on ethics. At first he refused but the dean of the law school encouraged him to accept. Tense, he approached his first week of classes in January. He read from his notes, eyes down. He dreamed one night that he was threatening the class: The congregations don't care. They'll use you. They won't cry if they destroy your family life or your marriage or your health. If you drop, they'll say it's your own fault and they'll replace you. They want you holy, they want you a workaholic, and they want you cheap. You're nothing to them. It's all nothing. It's Hell.

The next fall the divinity school requested the classes on ethics continue. Spencer sweated his way through the term.

"No more," he told the dean in December.

"Just the winter term, Spence, then we'll talk again."

"What is it you want me to teach them so badly?"

"Ethics. The law. The truth."

Spencer left the dean's office and walked off the campus to the seashore nearby. He slipped and stumbled along the beaches that gradually led him to the downtown area, near the docks and marinas. A wind tore at his face and at his overcoat. Salt water sloshed over his Oxfords and chilled his feet. Rain roared over his body and eyes.

"Where are the ships?" he asked a commissionaire.

"What ships, sir?"

"The carol ships. Where are the carol ships? It's Christmas in a few days."

"They won't be out tonight, sir. Too much wind. Too much rain. You might as well get yourself into a dry house. You won't hear a carol tonight."

Spencer went on into a tangle of bushes and sand and slippery rock. He tried to balance on a boulder and fell into the sea, the water closing over him. He struggled to the surface, spitting.

"There's nothing to say!" he shouted.

Waves slapped his mouth and nose and salt water burned down the back of his throat.

"If I'm honest it will just discourage them. Is that what you want?"

His body grew colder and colder.

"I can't hold their hands and go back into the churches with them!"

A foghorn groaned. Spencer splashed to the beach. He began to pick up stones and branches and arrange them in the sand. He scooped out holes and mounds. What began as something small expanded over ten or twelve feet. His fingers stiffened and blood from barnacle scrapes stained his skin.

"There, there, there," he grunted.

It was a creche. Village walls of stone and houses of stick covered by seaweed roofs, roads, hills with sheep fashioned from dead leaves, stickmen for shepherds, and down from the hills, down, down, a stable of rusted nails, no roof, jutting out of a sand slope, abundant magi with long green hair, Mary and Joseph out of shells and snails, animals of thistles, but what, what for the baby? What for the manger, what for his body, what for the incarnation? Sand, blood, mud, what, what to hail the agony of Christianity? Tinsel? Holly? Balloons?

Spencer broke a thorn branch in his hands, jerked off his tie to bind the pieces, pushed the cross into the middle of the stable, sucked the blood on his fingers and, hour after hour, watched the tide rise. It took everything, the roads, the houses, the shepherds, the magi, the animals, Mary, Joseph, the stable, it covered everything with its water and, as it ebbed in the muddy dawn, smoothed all, so that the sand was without blemish, rinsed clean and flawless as far as Spencer could see. All taken but one, the cross, crooked and stooped, Spencer's tie plastered to the sand like a weed. He put the cross in his pocket, where it stabbed him again.

Shivering, he found a coffee shop just up from the beach. The waitress stared at him as he sat down.

"Coffee?" she asked.

"Yes."

"Black?"

"Yes."

"Excuse me, sir, but are you all right? Can I get you a towel or something? You look terrible."

"Yes, of course I look terrible," Spencer grimaced from out of his bloodless face. "It's Christmas Eve, all the trees are dancing with plastic angels, I'm a believer, and it's been two thousand years. What should I look like?"

She poured his coffee, shrugged, turned to greet a man who came through the door with a grin and a shout.

"Hey, Amy! Merry Christmas! You going to be on the ships tonight?"

"I guess. Haven't missed in twenty years. You know, it's one of those days, Bill, I believe I could sing all night."

13

A Bookshop at the
End of Christendom

Bryanna loved books, read them before sleep, when told to turn off her light, did so and squirrelled under the blankets with a flashlight. She loved the outpouring of summer heat, played long and hard with the other boys and girls in her neighbourhood. But she longed for the rainy, overcast days when she did not have to go outside to play, for then she could take another book and climb into a corner of the attic in the midst of a herd of old trunks. (In her mind, she sat in tall African grass and around her, nothing to be alarmed about, squatted her sleeping elephants, her sentinels).

When God burst upon the scene she was astonished, not because she did not believe in God but because she did—she had not expected him to wish to become so personal. In the end, it turned out well enough. The best places for her to talk with him were elm groves, riverbanks, the quiet of her bedroom—or among the elephants in the attic. She and God got along fine. She gave him her love for books and he returned the love to her with a thought: Instead of becoming a pastor's wife (someone at her new church had mentioned this), why not own and manage her own bookshop?

It began modestly enough out of her parents' rec room while she was still working on her MA in English literature. Between seven and ten each week night she welcomed two or three people through sliding glass doors into a rec room bright with fresh pine shelving and coloured racks. There was a section for used books and texts, as well as a section of brand new titles. She offered a ten percent discount on every purchase. Her inventory was not large but it was not dull either. Word got around not only to students but began to percolate through the town's population, including the Christian community. She had a shelf or two for religious books, trying to select the most profound, the most thoughtful she had come across in her own reading, whether new titles or old. Not many were purchased. Her pastor had coffee with her and tactfully recommended a few contemporary Christian authors. She located the books mentioned, read them, did not find them to her taste, refused to stock them. What did it matter? This little basement shop was not so much a business as it was an intrigue, a passion, a blessing.

She pursued her PhD in literature. Her parents died. Her sister and brother wanted the house sold and the equity shared. She arranged to pay out their shares in the home but this placed a financial burden over her she had never experienced before. Suddenly, the volume of her weekly and monthly sales began to matter a great deal. Taking the plunge, she moved her stock out of the rec room into a retail outlet, walked through other bookstores, took notes, improved the scope of her inventory, and opened for business.

It quickly became apparent that in order to secure the Christian market more changes would have to be made. Persons from various churches would drop by looking for books on angels, on demons, on spiritual warfare, on the end of the world. Where were her titles? She showed them what she had: William of St. Thierry, Bernard of Clairvaux, Johann Arndt, Brother Lawrence, John Wesley, John Bunyan, Thomas à Kempis, John Calvin, Menno Simons, Theresa of Avila, John of the Cross, Philip Doddridge, Thomas Goodwin, C.S. Lewis' lesser known works...

No, no, no. Where were the Christian westerns and frontier sagas? Where were the romances, the big thick ones? And the books on the Anti-Christ and Armageddon, giving days and hours and accurate timetables? Where were the spiritual thrillers, where Christians took on houses full of demons and witches and Satanists? No, no, not those mysteries written by G.K. Chesterton about Father Brown or those ones by Dorothy Sayers about Lord Peter Whimsey. The new thrillers, the books with dark clouds and vicious bolts of lightning on their covers.

Had it been only one or two customers, Bryanna could have ignored it, which is what she intended to do. But the bank mumbled over her sales figures, hours could go by without a person in the store—except for the quaint, talkative types she loved who browsed but scarcely ever bought. Back in her attic, she prayed among the elephants and listened, but only heard the rustling of pigeon wings on the roof. Reluctantly, she developed a section pretty much overnight, just a small section, the best-sellers of contemporary Christendom, fiction and non-fiction.

People noticed and snapped the new titles up. She expanded the section. Soon it was generating more income than any other part of the store. A few of the quaint customers grumbled about the new section. She did not care for the books either but business was business. She had to make a living. Certain mornings, especially mornings when God struck fire in her soul, her spirit quailed when she unlocked the front door of the bookstore and was assaulted by lurid dust jackets of bursting bombs and rumbling tanks and the scowling faces of sinister world leaders—the Biblical Prophecy section—or she was brought up short by the flowing hair, air-brushed beauties of the Christian romances who looked like their counterparts on the local drugstore racks, except the Christian heroines were somehow purer and more angelic. Bryanna would steel herself to march past the rows of demons and the rows of angels on her way to the till. From this vantage point the worst eyesore was the area of how-to, self-help books: *How to Pray Like Jesus in Seven Days*; *Fasting and Praying for Financial Success*; *Self-Exorcism Overnight*; *Seven Sermons for Insomniacs*; *How to Build a Prosperous Christian Business and Expand Your Spiritual Influence*. The whole direction her store was taking spawned a ferocious warfare in her mind and soul. She knew she needed the money. Without the Christian book sales the bank would shut her down.

And what if they did? What difference did her store make? What sort of minds was she helping form, what sort of souls? Why not sell marshmallows instead of books and see if anybody noticed?

"I still have my section on Christian Classics. I stay open to sell them."

"Sell them? You couldn't give them away with any purchase under five dollars. Who bought the last one? Who?"

Bryanna punched out the code on her main till, refusing to answer the taunt from her warring mind.

"You did."

Some days she could ignore it. The hours passed in a blur, she had six staff, she could hide herself in her office if she wanted, to all appearances scanning her computer screen for special orders on Christian fitness videos—in fact, the one time someone peered over her shoulder, she was reading Bonhoeffer's *Cost of Discipleship* on CD-ROM.

The days she could not hide were the most stressful, usually when staff were ill or the Christmas crush was on. Then she had no choice but to face the onslaught that was late twentieth-century Christendom. Angel lapel pins for blessing and good fortune? Yes, sir, right over by the Jesus Is The Real Thing ball caps. *Losing Weight, Finding God?* Three left in hardcover in the Contemporary Christian Lifestyles section. Gregorian chants done as rap? Mainstream Christian Artists.

Sometimes she would snap and say whatever came into her head:

Look, she would plead, why this? Why a book on prayer written by a financial whiz and ex-football star? Why not this book here, by Metropolitan Anthony, Beginning to Pray? Slim, but lucid and full of wisdom.

Met. Mets? He's a ball player?

No, a leader in the Orthodox Church.

No, no, I need something by a strong Christian, someone who's still alive, who has a testimony, someone who's succeeded at something else besides Christianity and can talk to ordinary people about God, someone they'll listen to.

C.S. Lewis wrote this book also, ma'am.

Yes, well, was that before or after his conversion?

Oh, after. It's very good, very insightful.

All I need is a set of *The Chronicles of Narnia*. You have those, don't you? That's his best known work, isn't it?

George MacDonald also wrote these extremely interesting sermons.

No. I just need one of his romances.

Do you have a section on plays?

There are some over there. We also have T.S. Eliot and Dorothy Sayers in this section.

No. I need something people can understand, something written in the past year or two. Over there?

Yes. Over there.

In one of her darkest indulgences in self-destruction, she loaded her spiritual self-help section with books on plumbing, pouring concrete, roofing, wiring, caulking, and even set up a tool display. The books sold quickly, within a month the tool display with them.

"It goes well with the store," a customer encouraged her.

Her posture had always been firm and erect. As the years in the bookstore thundered over her head like a herd, she began to yield and bend. The more she fought expanding her store into a Christian retail outlet—Jesus watches, Mickey Mouse watches with Bible verses, rubber Christs and rubber crosses with magnets for the fridge—the more she yielded and the closer she seemed to slip towards the earth, the more her shoulders slumped with her neck, the more her gait became a shuffle: "I remind myself of Marley with manacles."

At 63 she sold the store to a huge Christian retail chain, paid off the loan from the bank and the mortgage on her parents' house, and disappeared. Six months later a new bookstore opened in the city, a small ad popping up in blue in the Yellow Pages. Its name was simply Queer Duck. The quaint ones who browsed much but bought little found the store soon enough. Yes, thank God, it was Miss Bryanna. A warm little shop from out of the storm. Others found her too, new customers who wandered up to the pale yellow house trimmed in white and opened the sliding glass doors. Grateful for the titles, they became her friends. Her pastor, now retired, shook his head. Obscure titles, obscure authors. She nodded and smiled, tall and straight as a white aspen, standing firmly behind a brown birch counter.

"Plenty of other stores have the popular ones," she responded.

"You won't make any money."

"I was thinking about helping people love God with their minds this week. Having a special."

"You're not being realistic, my dear."

"Perhaps I ought to extend the special to the end of my life."

"Bryanna! And you ought to think about changing the name of your bookstore. It's bound to offend, turn some away."

"I rather like my life again, pastor. I expect I'll leave my shop this way unless God drops Job, Ecclesiastes, and the Song of Solomon from his own best-seller."

She died in the shop one summer night that was full of crickets and moon. A pale arm was draped over the birch counter like a long thin taper, and her hair had unravelled and fallen over her face and features like gentle snow. Not surprisingly, the other hand held a book. She had been reading a paperback that looked brand new but had the cover design of a pocketbook from the 1930s or the 1940s—part of her old stock of Christian classics she had found discarded in a dumpster a few days after the book chain had purchased her store. They tried to slide the book out from under her hand but eventually had to pry it loose from her tenacious fingers: Thomas à Kempis, *The Imitation of Christ*. A friend thought it best to cremate the book with Bryanna.

14

Our Saviour's picture
not made with hands

It was a storm that gnarled over the new building, torrents thick as
ships' cables hurled from the roof. The building was large, the parking lot larger, empty and flooding, oil rainbows falling at the curb,
draining into the dark under the street. Walls and walls and slabs of
roof. The man in the long black Australian riding coat, rivers bent and
twisting over the oiled cloth to the road, thought at first that he was
mistaken. He hesitated. It seemed to him a space enclosing the head
offices of a major corporation. Impersonal, functional, without a history, it waited for him, indifferent to his decision. Long cars began to
pull into the shining black lot, lights glittering, wipers rhythmic with
other wipers. He glanced at the entrance they came driving through.
There was a minute black cross and some tidy lettering etched on an
opaque white surface: Holy Rose Tabernacle. Now he looked more
closely at the roof above the brass and oak and smoked glass doors.
There was a slight swelling and a faint cross. He pushed against the
heavy doors and was encased in carpet and the smell of fresh paint and
a silence that had no sound. His coat hung, he came through another
set of heavy doors into the sanctuary, a scented hand pressed his, he
took the bulletin to his blue-padded pew, all around him the bleached
oak gleamed and there were long slats of windows tinted red and green
and yellow, and the rain was unheard. There was only a person cough-

ing. Soon the organ found and filled every corner of the space.

"We thank the Lord for this building. We want to bless it this evening. And we want all of you to contribute to its holy beauty. So the Church Council would love to see your paintings, your drawings, art that brings glory to God. If you could bring your pieces in this Wednesday evening for Pastor Grace and Pastor Leviathan and the elders to look at, well, that would be wonderful. Let's all be a part of this. Let's adorn in beauty and humility the house of the Lord. Amen?"

At home that afternoon the man, his long black coat drying on a hook by the back door of the house, bent over a panel of birchwood about two feet by one foot. He passed his long white fingers over it. Smooth enough. From a pot at his elbow he spread on a layer of gesso, like a plaster. Then he laid white canvas on this, rubbing, rubbing until the canvas was the wood. He spread more gesso. He went into another room to read a book. When he returned, the gesso had hardened. So he polished it like a bone or a precious stone. He coaxed a gleaming out of it. An old book was propped up by the table lamp. With a fine brush dipped in scarlet paint he began to trace a pattern over the white surface, consulting the book occasionally. Then, with another brush, he fashioned the background into a more startling whiteness, as if one had walked out into sun sudden on a snowfall. He returned to his book in the other room. At two in the morning the panel was dry. From a drawer he brought out a set of paints in an old wooden tray splotched as though someone had bled. He had carried a cool brown egg from the fridge. Cracking it quickly, he juggled the shells in his fingers, the golden yolk slipping into one glass bowl, the white of the egg into a green ceramic dish. The shells fell at his feet, broken steadily through the night by the black shoes on his feet, again and again, the fragments becoming as fine as a sand. He used the yolk to dilute his paints, one at a time. Carefully brushing the paints onto the panel, the colours fired like the sun, moon and stars, the egg's yolk giving them radiance and a strength, a firm opaqueness, the deep of the morning.

It was impossible to stop once begun. At noon of the following day, having stooped over the panel through the raining night, he quickly ate some bread and made some tea, then returned to the pool of light on the table and the colours swirling and rising. Paint spotted the skin on his fingers and hands and arms, smudges jumped onto his forehead and cheeks, the stubble on his chin darkened, his eyes marbled with fine red cracks.

At the meeting at the new church building on Wednesday night the man did not appear. Thirty others did with sketches and watercolours and needlepoint. Not wishing to offend, the Council found a wall or a nook for everything. But there was a great blank wall just before people entered the sanctuary.

"We'll hang a picture of the pastors," thought one elder.

Pastors Grace and Leviathan said nothing.

"Or," another suggested, "we can buy a large print of the Last Supper from the Christian bookstore."

"No, no," a third argued, "that's grim stuff. We're going in there to worship. Something lighter, happier."

"Jesus on a seashore."

"Jesus with a lamb."

"Jesus sleeping. In a boat."

"Well," suggested Pastor Leviathan, "let's just pray about it and see."

They turned off the lights and went home.

By Sunday morning, a painting had appeared, colour, colour, colour on stabbing white, only two feet by one foot, but seeming to stretch out to cover the entire naked wall.

Pastor Leviathan said nothing. He thought Pastor Grace had hung it. Pastor Grace said nothing. She thought Pastor Leviathan and the Council had agreed to it on her day off. The elders said nothing. They each thought the others had agreed to it over the weekend.

The silence could not last long. The painting was disturbing. It forced your eyes to it, seized your mind, struck against your heart. Persons complained to the elders, or at least, several of the elders declared that many people had done so.

"Half the church," one declared at a special meeting later in the week.

"Well, who agreed to put it up?" asked Pastor Leviathan.

"Didn't you?" This from Pastor Grace.

"I wasn't invited to any meeting," growled one elder.

"Who put it up?"

"Pastor Grace?"

"I haven't been in the church since our meeting Wednesday night. I've been doing visitation."

"You mean someone just came in and put it up without authority?"

"Is there a name on it?"

They rushed out to the foyer. There was no signature on the front. They took it down. Nothing on the back.

"It's an original."

"How can you tell?"

"Well, it's down now. Let's keep it down."

"Where will we put it?"

"In the church basement."

Everyone felt uneasy about this.

"After all, even if we don't like it, it's still a religious painting."

"Does someone want to take it home?"

No one did.

"Listen, I'm hungry," said Pastor Leviathan. "Let's store it in my office. We'll find out who it belongs to on Sunday."

He placed it carefully, leaning the painting against the wall so the image could not be seen.

It was overcast as they finally made their way to the parking lot. They opened the doors of their long cars.

"What was the painting of anyway?" asked an elder as she removed her key from the lock.

Pastor Leviathan sat behind his steering wheel and shrugged.

"I think," offered Pastor Grace, taking a mint from her purse, "that it is far away and hard to be sure, but I think it is the Crucifixion."

After the next Sunday service they were forced to have an impromptu meeting inside Pastor Leviathan's office. The painting was still propped image towards the wall. The men hunched forward in their seats, the ladies sat upright, legs crossed.

"Half the church," said one elder firmly.

"They want it back up?"

"Yes."

"Why?"

"One said it woke her up. It gave her spiritual thoughts."

"Jim Evans said it helped his focus."

"Evans? The lawyer?"

"He said it was strong."

"I don't know who all you've been talking to. Marsha McKenzie was glad it was gone. She offered to do a needlepoint of Psalm 150. Praising God in his sanctuary. I'm telling you, that makes a lot more sense to me than a crucifixion."

"I'm afraid I have to go with Bill. A lot of people asked me why it was gone. Carla Stones wanted to know who thought they had the right to remove a sacred object from a church?"

There was a silence. Pastor Leviathan's stomach rumbled. He cracked his knuckles quickly to cover the sound up.

A man in a long black riding coat opened the door.

"Excuse me?" he asked.

"We are having a meeting, I'm sorry." Pastor Leviathan rose from his chair.

"Is it about the image?" the man asked.

"Are you a visitor? Perhaps we could get together for coffee during the week?"

"I know who put up the image."

"Perhaps," said Pastor Grace after a silence, "you could join us."

The man came into the room but did not sit.

"Is there a problem?" he asked.

"If you know who painted it, tell him it's too harsh," said one elder.

"Yes. It's unpleasant. You don't drive all the way to church on a Sunday morning for that."

"It doesn't prepare you for worship. It jangles your nerves. I need to be calmed."

"The week is bad enough without seeing some guy hanging off a cross."

"That's Jesus," Pastor Grace broke in, "that's Jesus on the cross, Tom."

"It's a picture. How do we know who it is? Everything's too far away. The painting doesn't even look like a photograph. It isn't true to life."

"We still have a lot of people who want a picture up. What are we going to do about that?"

"The Christian bookstore ..."

"They don't want a ten cent print from the bookstore."

"A lot of them liked the fact that it was an original. Painted by one of our own people."

"Who did paint it?"

They looked at the man in the long coat. Pastor Grace noticed that he was growing a beard and was in that scruffy stage before a beard filled in nicely.

"Perhaps," the man responded, "another image would suit you better."

Pastor Leviathan grunted. "If you can get your friend to make another one. It would be a great blessing."

"Yes. Another one. Toned down."

"A biblical theme. Something from the gospels."

"Something peaceful."

"Something to get people in the mood to worship."

"Something with compassion."

The man nodded. "I will look into it."

He went out the door.

"Who is that, Pastor Grace?"

"I don't know him."

"Well, let's hope he has some influence on this painter."

"Perhaps the new picture will be up for Sunday."

"What are you going to do with the old one?"

Pastor Leviathan loosened his tie. "I don't know."

"You could throw it out."

"No."

"You could sell it. We could use the money to finish off the kitchen before the Christmas banquet."

"I can't sell it."

"Why not?"

"I'm just going to leave it alone."

Sunday came. A new painting on birchwood hung from the long plaster wall. Persons walking up to the sanctuary doors noticed it immediately. A mother of three said it reached out and grasped her hand. A small boy thought it was alive. Jim Evans, the lawyer, was smiling in anticipation when he approached it, ceased to smile, went slowly into the sanctuary, brooded. He did not rise at any time during the service. When he shook Pastor Grace's hand at the door, he said, "It's in me."

There was yet another meeting that Wednesday night. This time it was in Pastor Grace's office. She sat behind her desk. A half-moon shone through the vertical blinds at her back.

"Look. I like pictures as much as anyone," began one elder. "I have two or three prints by Norman Rockwell. And one of a Spitfire over England. And a wolf, a Bateman. I love the stuff. But it fits. Do you know what I mean? It goes with the flow. I've got my TV and my books and my leather armchair. And it all goes together. The pictures aren't obtrusive. They're exactly right, add to the atmosphere, make you feel good. But this! These pictures we keep getting. It's like being shot full of arrows. The colours are too bright and everything is too big."

"Like someone going after you with a hammer."

"Like someone going after you with a hammer. I come to church to find God and I find these paintings. They're upsetting. I'd go by them with my eyes rooted to the floor if I wasn't afraid of walking into the wall."

"I don't find it so bad. Why should it blend in with anything? Why can't it speak? Why can't Christ be noticed?"

"It's not Christ, it's a picture of Christ."

"How do you know it's Christ? All you see is an arm and a shadow."

"It's not natural. The style isn't natural. It doesn't look like our world."

"You have impressionist art up on your wall, Gunter."

"What?"

"The lily pads. Monet."

"You know they're lily pads."

"People hated his art. No one could tell what it was. You had to stand back, get distance. But you wanted to get pulled into all the colour and the layers of paint."

"You know they're lily pads."

"And you know what this painting is about."

"It doesn't look like anything in this world."

"You know what it's about."

"It doesn't look anything like I'd imagine."

"The paintings are distracting. People look at them. They talk about them. They don't have their minds on God."

"What do you mean? I find the new picture makes me think precisely about God."

"It's becoming an idolatry."

"Tom. People talk about hockey in the foyer a lot more than they talk about God. You don't call that idolatry."

"It's not trying to take the place of God."

"They are just pictures, for heaven's sake. Can we just calm down? These are nothing more than the products of someone's imagination. Some people like them, some don't. It's not a big deal."

"They're sacred."

"They're wood and paint."

"I don't like them. They're strange and they make me feel out of sorts."

"Let's just get rid of them. Let's be done with it."

"I enjoy this one. It's strong. It's good. You go in thinking about praying after you've looked at it, instead of sitting in the pew wondering what you ought to do after the service."

"I don't need a graven image to help me pray."

"You've got art up all over your house. A plate with some sort of head of Jesus on it."

"I don't pray to it."

"No one prays to the one on the wall here. Jesus isn't even on it, so what is the problem? We have all that other art up too. What about all the drawings and the needlepoint?"

"Nobody says anything about that stuff except that it's nice. It blends in. This painting jumps out at you. It doesn't fit. We need an atmosphere. The painting shouldn't be noticed. All your faith should be in your head and your head should be clear, no pictures, no imagining, no idolatry, just like a clear running stream, fresh and translucent."

"We watch TV and we watch movies but we can't have a painting in church?"

"We don't worship TV. And TV isn't strong like this. It doesn't stay with you. But these paintings. They need to be muted."

"The church," said Pastor Leviathan, "is rattling with spirituality."

Pastor Grace nodded. "I have to agree. There is an intensity. The praying, the worship, the way people follow the sermons."

"Thank God. Praise God. But don't praise the paintings."

"We have bread and wine," mused Pastor Leviathan, "we have steeples and crosses and Sunday School pictures of Jesus. We pin doves to our suit lapels. Banners are going to hang in the sanctuary this Christmas. There will be a nativity scene. Advent candles in a circle."

"That is all normal. The paintings are dangerous."

"Shall we split the church over them?" demanded Pastor Grace.

"If we take this one down too, what will the congregation say?"

"Some will be glad. Very, very glad."

"And the others?"

Pastor Leviathan stood up. "The painter's friend. I asked him to drop by. I think I heard him come in."

He stepped out and brought the man into the office. His beard looks better, thought Pastor Grace.

"Can your friend not do something simple?" asked an elder.

"Such as?" responded the man.

"Not a scene. Not a story. Something basic."

"Like a painting of the Jordan."

"Or Jerusalem."

"Flowers."

"A simple head. Moses. John the Baptist. Paul."

"An angel."

"Perhaps," said Pastor Grace, "that would be common ground for all of us here. Hopefully common ground for the entire church. Your friend wants to help our church, doesn't he?"

"Yes."

"We need common ground. Ask your friend to paint something that's straight forward, that isn't controversial, something everyone can agree on."

"I will see what can be done."

"We should like to meet the painter."

"I will see what can be done."

The man left. Pastor Grace closed the meeting with a prayer and they moved into the foyer. The painting was there on the wall. One of the elders, his face a blank, went over and removed it, trying to keep it from touching his body. He handed it to Pastor Leviathan.

"I don't want to see it again," the elder warned. "You should destroy it."

Pastor Leviathan waited until the others had left the building. He went into his office. He did not turn on the light. Moonbeams stroked his face and hands, the walls. He stared at the small painting in his hand. A leper. Skin in shreds. Desperately reaching out a hand. And a hand taking his, holding on tightly. There was no body or face to the hand. Only a shadow. You assumed it was Jesus. There was hope in the paint, in the leper's eyes, in the strangeness as strange as life, in the moon, there in the office, something was opening. He hung the painting of the leper so that it would face him directly as he sat at his desk. Then he lifted the other painting away from the wall. In the dark and in the light the skin glistened, the arms pulsed, the blood moved down the wood, down the tree, down to the earth. But it was all far away and the body had no face. The head was in the shadows. Surely it was Jesus. Overhead, the angels' wings beat, a soft thudding in the air. He placed the painting so it would always be at his back, as if to grant him strength and purpose. He sat down at his desk and let the paint and the images surround him. In the course of time, the moon left the sky. He sat in a throbbing dark.

Sunday was a sky that had not made up its mind. Banks of cloud spilled grey and white and purple over the edge, wind knotted grass clippings and green elm leaves and dust, the sun struggled and people bent their heads as they came across the parking lot broad as a plain. Coats and jackets were stripped off and hung, men and women brushed and combed their hair at mirrors, children raced in and out of the washrooms, there were greetings, heads nodded, sharp laughs, a straightening of ties and silk scarves. Then people moved towards the sanctuary. Ushers waited for them at the large oak double doors. Their feet came soundlessly across the carpet. To the wall.

Some glanced, walked on quickly, took a bulletin, shook an usher's hand, found their pew. Others stood and gazed. Whoever came by grew silent. The children's freedom sounded so much greater in this sudden quiet before the sanctuary.

"Johnny, that's enough, stop it."

"Sarah-Jane, lower your voice, we're in church."

"Shh. Shh."

They streamed past, six, seven hundred of them, stopping, staring, walking on, lingering, entering the sanctuary in a hush.

"I want to pray today, I want to pray," announced Pastor Leviathan from behind the oak pulpit, massive as a ship's prow. "Can we do that for five minutes? Not one minute or two. Five minutes of silence. Can we pray?"

So the organ and the hymns and hundreds of voices and the fluttering of Bible pages and Pastor Grace wrestling with the words of her sermon, stretching out to the wood, the nails, and the leper, and the end of the sevice coming in whiteness and in quiet, the quiet of anger, the quiet of grief, the quiet of night and morning.

They assembled by common consent in Pastor Leviathan's office. Several were too restless to sit.

"That's it, that's enough," said one elder. "Either the paintings stop or I'm pulling my family out."

"The paintings are ruining our church. We used to be a happy, friendly congregation. Now we come into the sanctuary like a pack of monks. Everyone is so serious and so intense it makes me sick."

"You think it's the paintings?"

"I know it's the paintings. We're all normal when we come in the front door. Then we walk up to that wall and it destroys us. We stop talking, we stop laughing. That's not from God."

"I agree. The paintings have become the central focus."

"They're dominating everything else we do."

"They're idols."

"A lot of people think that. They're sick of looking at this grotesque imagery every Sunday they come to worship. We're hindering their freedom."

"Half the church."

"What about all the others who love the stuff?" asked Pastor Leviathan.

"Let them hang the things in their bedrooms if they want. But not in the house of the Lord. This is a place of worship for everyone. We can't keep catering to a few airy fairies."

"Come off it, Tom. You're going to call Jim Evans an airy fairy?"

"We have pictures of what Jesus is supposed to look like in every Sunday School room. Are we making our kids worship idols?"

"No one takes those pictures seriously."

"What are you saying?"

"They're peripheral. The ones in front of the sanctuary stop you dead."

"You want a Jesus of water, a Jesus like milk."

"I do. Jesus is the Word and I want the milk of the Word, just like it says in the Bible. I want what's normal. What's biblical."

"Our lives are full of pictures. Why can't our sacred pictures have some substance to them? Some colour?"

"I want my mind clear."

"You fill it with everything else. But Jesus has to be a blank."

"Clear water."

"No. A glass of tepid milk."

"These paintings are not more important than the harmony of our congregation. It's imagination, just someone's imagination. The paintings aren't real. They're fluff, lies, water and wood and pigment. But our people—they're made in the image of God."

"We can imagine things and create things. Isn't that like God? What are sermons but thin air without our imaginations?"

"I am not going to stay and keep this up week after week."

"Our church is getting ripped apart."

"I thought we were finding God. This morning was incredible."

"This morning was a joke. A bunch of long faces."

"Take them down. Let the wall be blank. No faces and bodies screaming for your attention. Just purity. Emptiness. Clear of everything. A spiritual worship."

"Are we agreed to take these paintings down once and for all?" asked Pastor Leviathan.

No one answered.

"I'll remove it," he said, standing up.

"Not to go into your office like these others. We won't have it in this building, pastor. This painting was the final blasphemy. I'll put the thing where it belongs. The sooner we get back to normal in this church, the better."

The elder thumped out of the office, tore the painting from the wall, and strode to a side exit, a steel door. Opening it, a gust drenched him. Tie askew, hair flapping about his head, he tried to cram the painting into a metal garbage bin. But the bin was full. He attempted to break the wooden panel over his knee but he slipped and fell, ripping a pant leg. He cursed and hurled the painting across the lane against the side of a building. Colour scraped onto the pale bricks. The painting lay face-up in the storm.

Some time later, near dark, the man in the long black coat came by, looked down at the image, but would not touch it. Three times he made the sign of the cross over it and then walked on, drooping, swept by gales.

When the darkness arrived in its fullness, a light came on over the church's side door, casting a thin sheen over the painting. And the door opened and Pastor Leviathan came and stood in the storm and gazed down at the eyes and the skin but he would not touch it either, nor bring it back into the building, and he left it there and returned to the warmth and light and comfort of the church, slowly closing the steel door behind him.

For a long time nothing more happened, only the rain and the dark and the yellow light. But in the dead of night an elderly lady came, dressed in tattered coats, scarves wound about her head, pushing a shopping cart filled with bottles and cans and rotting fruit and cardboard, somehow managing to keep a cigarette lit between her narrow lips. Clattering she came, stopping at the church's garbage bin. Rummaging through it, she found nothing, just wads of Sunday School papers bright with pictures of Jesus, and some others showing various artisans building and decorating the Temple in Jerusalem. Rain and wind swept these out into the night, plastering several firmly onto the asphalt and the muck. Puffing her cigarette in disgust, she let the bin's lid slam shut. Just before she pushed her cart over it, she saw the painting. She stooped in the weak light and squinted.

Cigarette smoke a white mist over her head, she brushed raindrops from the face of Christ, from the forehead and thorns and lips. Grunting, she picked him up and placed him face-up in the cart, on top of all the cans and bottles and cardboard. Humming and puffing, she rattled ahead down the long black lane, the image balanced precariously, the rain, the raining, running, running like blood, and the eyes.

15

Mister Good Morning

There were two gardens, he said. One at the beginning of the world and another at the end. Both beautiful. Both overflowing with the kind of life and fecundity only things green and rooted and flowering and spangled with rain can give. To breathe in is to breathe in the soul of God. To breathe out is to exhale the Incarnation. Mister Buon Giorno we called him, because he was as warm and mellow as a prairie summer sunrise, and because he was Italian. Mister Good Morning.

But that sort of talk came later. In the beginning was a tumour of weeds, especially the Scotch thistle, with its purple crown and its agony to anyone who handled it without gloves. Rocks. A rusted spade, brown and crumbly as demerara sugar. Chaos—a yard of hidden darkness sown with tin cans and chip packages and splinters of glass. The whole earth lumped and cracked and, in a rain wind, grey and black as a cold pail of ash. The fence tired and sagging, letting anything come and go, fed up. The house was a normal white stucco with a dead brown roof and dead brown window trim. I passed by this house and the yard a thousand times, seeing nothing, my mind on where I was going. I finally noticed the yard when I fell into it from a tall crab apple tree.

It was Old Man Reynolds' tree. His house, white and blue and sturdy, dominated one end of our block. His backyard was green with leaves and apples and grass. The fence was white and solid. And there, on the other side of it, was the chaos. Reynolds' yard, on the other hand, was paradise. A crab apple Eden. And it was we who, succumbing to temptation, took and ate.

Not that Reynolds let us get it without a fight. The back door could fly open, a blaze of light, the joy of fear running up the stairs in our chests, our shirts and pockets bumpy with the little apples, jumping, racing, laughing, while Old Man Reynolds thundered to the gate and harried us into darkest night, illumined by only a few gleaming street lamps: "You leave my apple trees alone!"

Once he'd clearly had enough and was determined to make a kill. We ran with the legs of eleven- and twelve-year-olds, pronghorns, and he raged after us down the back lane, through the yards, almost over a seven-foot fence. A hand that had seen many summers gnarled over the edge of this fence, a foot popped over, there was the promise of the whole enraged beast, and we continued to pelt across the yard into another back lane. But the hand trembled on the wood, the shoed foot strained, there was a shout, both hand and foot disappeared, a crashing and a rolling and a silence. Old Man Reynolds limped back to Crab Tree Castle.

We hooted. We cheered. But, in actuality, I saw none of this. When the wrath of Reynolds had blazed all around us, I had been so startled I toppled backwards over the fence into the yard of darkness. Scotch thistles eagerly speared my back and legs and tore their nails across my eyes and mouth. The little apples spilled out over the crusted earth. I felt Reynolds blunder down the lane after the others like a snorting buffalo bull. Suddenly there was a jabbing pain in my elbow. A rock. I tried to roll over and I thrust my hand in fierce glass that happily drew my blood. More thorns spiked my face. I stopped moving. I heard Reynolds come back. He went into his house and returned with a flashlight, playing it over his yard, spitting out hard, short words as he examined the branches stripped of fruit and leaf. The beam passed over my body and I saw the blood on my fingers. Then his door thumped shut.

"That crazy yard!" I steamed to the others later. "I'm going to fix it."

"What about the owners?"

"No one owns it. The house is empty. The Shanks moved out in the spring."

"Somebody bought it."

"Well. They're not here yet. I'm going to clean up that mess so we can use the yard for hiding. Who wants to help?"

I wound up hacking at the weeds on my own, imagining I was battling an army, one kilted, thorny Scot falling after another, in the dark, no moon, just like the war movies I watched. I had Dad's working gloves, some old jeans, a Levi's jacket. After the weeds, I chopped at the soil with a pick, always hitting stone, the shock burning my arms, water blisters leaping up on my palms, the glass cut biting under its bandage. The next time I raided the crab apple trees I would leap onto soft soil, crouching like a panther. I put aside the pick for a spade, shoving it in with my runnered foot, turning the rough soil over.

"You are beginning a garden?"

I dropped my shovel and was sure it was Old Man Reynolds. I was about to spring over the broken fence. But the voice was not Reynolds' and the man was too small.

"You are a good boy to do this work for me. It always breaks my back. And under the stars! You are a romantic."

He came closer and knelt, both knees, in the bit of earth I had cleared and turned. He took up handfuls and rubbed them against his face.

I still wanted to run. "I'm sorry," I said. "I didn't know you lived here." I began to clink and clatter the tools together and head for the fence.

"Smell this, eh?" In the darkness he held darkness. "Under all of that rubbish, black soil, Red River soil, I can grow everything with this. Come."

He took the hoe from me and he began whacking at the weed bushes. "Keep on. You are welcome here." Hesitantly, I began to shove in the spade with my foot once again. After thirty minutes he said it was enough. I still had not seen his face clearly.

"Tomorrow is Saturday. Come tomorrow and I will give you lunch. Bring your tools."

In five years I would be thinking his voice was black olives and piazzas and warm winds and Mediterranean waters, for by then I would have travelled to Caserta and Perugia and Roma and Assisi for myself. That night I thought he might be Polish or Dutch. He shook my hand. His skin was burning. I went down the lane three houses to my own place, leaned the fork and spade and hoe and pick against the back wall, gazed up at the gusts of summer stars, no moon, bright water beads on a black coat sleeve. I did not want to go in and sleep, for that would be an ending.

We cleared the entire yard the next day and turned every foot of the rigid soil. Rocks were heaped in one corner of the yard, weeds in another.

"Let them rot," he said, spraying the dead thistles and dandelions and chickweed with a hose. "Soon they will change their minds and help us. They will grow beans and tomatoes and squash."

The lunch was a salad, heavier to hold in my bowl than anything Mother made, full of things I would have refused at home—green olives, hot red peppers, spinach, misshapen white chunks of feta cheese. All drenched in olive oil and wine vinegar. There was a crusty heel of narrow white bread. I sat with him under the June sun and ate it all, wiping my bowl with the bread like he did.

"Good? Eh?"

"Yes."

"But nothing. How old is the spinach? How old are the peppers? They drive them up from Mexico and California before they are even ripe. In August, you will feast like a king. Everything will be fresh. You will taste something then."

The following Saturday was the fence. We knocked down the old, pounded in the new, a lattice of cedar wood he had me stain a burgundy red. While I flicked the brush he began to set up poles. Then he dug furrows. A sack lying on the earth produced a mound of seed packages and some dark bottles.

"What's in those bottles?" I asked.

"Seeds I have kept in the dark. Finish the fence and come."

There were rows zig-zagging all over the black earth. Beans, peas, zucchini, corn, broccoli.

"We are starting a month late," he said, "but we will be all right. We will have a hot September. And what do your Father and Mother plant?"

"Potatoes. Beets. Carrots. Peas. Green beans. Dill."

"Ah. Dill. Here, over here we will sow the herbs. So many bees will come."

July I spent at summer camp, shooting arrows, banging away with .22 rifles, riding horses, canoeing, hurling myself into food fights. When

I returned to our street in August, I had that young feeling of being older and wiser and a force to be reckoned with. I came down the back lane one morning heading for the bus stop.

"Buon giorno!" he called.

The yard was a forest. Beans raced scarlet up poles. Thick green leaves swarmed over the earth. A grape vine knotted itself along the lattice fence. Arbours had been built, offering gateways in and out of various parts of the garden, and they hung with zucchini and cucumbers. Flagstone laced through the bursting green. I was sure I recognized carrots and beets. The discarded rocks in the corner had been mounded in earth and rearranged, interspersed with blossoming plants, most with pink or white flowers, which he told me were herbs, and he named each one. The bees were all over them.

When I came into the yard I felt I was entering another country. Vines dangled over my head, brushing my hair. I stepped through an arbour and was overcome by colours and scents that left me bewildered. I found an old wooden bench and sat down. My new-found summer confidence evaporated. Dark plants pressed against me.

"Here."

It was a cherry tomato. I never ate tomatoes. I took it and tossed it in my mouth at once. The juice was sweet. The tomatoes in Mother's salad were pink. Why were these like dripping blood?

He sat beside me, drinking a glass of water, offering me one.

"There is much more to do," he nodded, "but the birds have already begun to come. Look. Robins. But it is the meadowlark I want. Over there are some seed bushes he should like. How is your parents" garden?"

"Very neat and tidy."

"Gardens must have a rhythm, that's true, but they should also be discoveries. You should make people search. I still need to build a pond, a fountain, some running water. I ought to have St. Francis of Assisi. Francesco. But not as a birdbath. I think, kneeling, and a stream passing from his cupped hands. Do you go to church?"

"Anglican."

"So you know the Holy Bible very well and all about the saints."

"I guess."

"Eden is the first garden, emerging out of the dark." He took bread and cheese from a pack by his feet and carved off large portions for

111

both of us. "Then there is the whole of life. We lose Eden. But God brings us back to paradise at the end. So this is my garden. Two Edens. Look."

He pointed with his knife at two rows of saplings I had not noticed. "Dwarf cherries. Twelve. And the stream must run down between them. You read the Holy Bible in your church, don't you? The river of God. The leaves of the trees are for the healing of the world. God walks in the garden with us again. Genesis. And the Revelation of St. John. The Apocalypse. So this is the idyllic. The perfect ending. You enter through that arbour and you are in Eden. Then you walk over there, you see, and you are expelled—I have some plants with strong odours and grim faces. But there, that other arbour, you step through the river of God and the trees are all about you, you are safe. Heaven. The garden is all one piece. Do you see that? The expulsion is our lives. It is only a moment."

I dreamed of his head, his face, exactly as it was, truer than it was. Dark hair around the back and sides. Ears tight to the head. A sharp dome of a skull. Eyes and eyebrows as if they were part of his garden, thick, hidden, a steady light, silver light, growing light. Small, smiling lips. He was planted, rooted, growing upward. Like his bean shoots or his scarves of lettuce. Black the soil from which he rose.

Summer could not end this garden. Fall crops fought up out of autumn death, kale green as the sea, curling over brown and orange leaves he let the wind blow in and out of Eden and back and forth through Heaven. "There is," he said as we drank tea together in October, "no end to God." I never drank tea."

The snows ought to have ended it. They were early that year, before Hallowe'en, whitening the world. Cold pressed against our faces and our homes. Christmas Eve I returned with my family from St. Mark's Anglican. We took a shortcut down the back lane. The arbours were rimmed with ice and brilliant with silver lights. And there were other lights. All along the fence. In the dwarf cherry trees. Smaller lights strewn over the snow on the ground, as if it were a seeding. The whole lane shone.

"Look at that," my Father said.

"He has some new evergreens there," observed Mother. "And a Colorado blue spruce. Silver lights and thick snow. He must be a charming man."

"The guy's a nut," my brother laughed.

"Shut up!" I shot.

"Do you two want to spend Christmas in the basement?" demanded Father.

Spring came in a hurry in March. The sun wasted no time. Snow melted quickly and the street flooded. The garden became a lake. Two mallards kicked lazily about. He laughed, the water over his boots, and threw them bread crumbs.

"Why not? I have my pond."

The planting was in May. He asked me to join him.

"I'm alone," he grunted as he pounded in a pole. "It's too big a country, eh? Vancouver. Calgary. Montreal. Halifax. My children are all over. But you will meet them this summer."

July took me to another camp. When I returned, Eden had burst full-grown from the earth, St. Francis bent and pouring water along a bed of coloured stones. I saw it at night, a half-moon giving enough light to see the leaves turning over and over in the warm wind. Traffic raced on the main street one house away. But when I opened the gate and stood within all the growing and flowing I might as well have been up a mountain slope in the Rockies for all the city noise that penetrated. I sat on a bench and breathed in. I recognized chive and fennel and strawberry. Heaped against his house were banks of flowers. I got up and went to them. The smell was a shock. I was used to pushing my nose into flowers when someone insisted and scenting nothing, having to pretend. The wind rolled the breath of the blossoms over me like dark purple breakers.

"Buon giorno!" he called the next day, the sun finding him under the deep green and putting gold to his arms. Two men and a woman sat with him in shorts and T-shirts. "Come. This is Franky. Anthony. And Carolina. This is the boy who has been helping me."

They laughed all through that morning I was with them. They shared their lunch, an evergreen sheltering us from a hot yellow sun. Salad, fish, chicken. Grape juice spotted with the petals of orange and white pansies.

"Eden, you see," he nodded. "Heaven. God walks with us. He

crushes the sage between his fingers. So we can smell it."

I helped him with the harvest along with his children. I was picking the cucumbers, reaching around mirrors to gently release them from their stalks.

"Doesn't this place cheer you up?" smiled Carolina, her hair and eyes dark as the soil that grew the garden.

"Yes."

"You seem so sullen. Excuse me."

I shrugged and picked smaller cucumbers for pickles.

"It's none of my business. Here. Have a strawberry. We are all grateful you've become our father's friend. He misses us. Mother's been gone two years now. But it's a big country. What can we do? He's seventy this birthday. Tomorrow. Come over. I have some special ice cream."

There was a centre to the garden where red bricks had been laid in a swirl and the brick right in the middle was etched with the name ROSA. There was lasagna and a pasta salad tossed with anchovies and a grilled salmon. It was a very loud time. The ice cream was good, swift and sweet in my throat.

"I have no meadowlarks, Tony," he said. And later, to Carolina, glancing down, "The garden where God walks. Heaven. So Rosa is there now. She holds seeds I cannot sow here. Holds plants I can never touch. Good for her." He wiped his eye and drank from a glass of water bobbing with lemon wedges. "I still do not have the pond," he turned to Franky, "and I do not have the meadowlark. But soon, I pray."

"It's time for Mass, Papa," Carolina announced, standing up.

"Ah. You can come with us."

I shook my head.

"I'd better go home."

"You are welcome."

"I'll see you next week. It was great to celebrate your birthday. It's been great to meet all of you."

The garden was eternal. Fall, winter, it remained, growing, sparkling with lights, all the other yards dark, Old Man Reynolds dead and the crab trees chopped down by a younger man who wanted a swimming pool. I imagined flying over the city by night and in the pool of darkness seeing Mister Good Morning's lights climbing up to heaven.

Several times when it was cold and late I came in through the back gate and left my bootprints in the snow. I swept off the bench and sat. Once it began to snow so softly, it was as if a flock of trumpeter swans had silently flown over, shedding long feathers that turned slowly and came to rest across the backs of my hands. Breathe in the breath of God, he said. Breathe out the flesh grafted to God. Care for God's garden. A privilege. Stoop down with him. Weed. Sow. Water. Harvest. Eat. Drink. Pray. Laugh. You see? All his plants, his herbs, his flowers. From Eden to Eden. The beginning of the Holy Bible, the end of the Holy Bible. Peace. Healing. Do you see?

Nothing changed except that I grew and the herbs grew and the evergreens grew and he created a pond and stocked it with goldfish and the sun rose and set and some winters the wind blew with a kind of madness and made the lights dance.

I took the train to Acadia University and I grasped a paper bag of vegetables and fruit in my lap. "This is your garden as much as mine," he said. "Visit me when you come back."

I returned at Christmas to a creche in the garden, dotted with fallen needles and oak leaves, blue lights pure over the sequined snow. I did not see him. There was a white candle in my pocket. Lit, the candle stood tall over the ice and the angels, patterns changing Jesus, Mary, Joseph, the shepherds, the magi, dark to light to dark. It burned quickly, guttered, the snow about it scorched and stained with the melted wax. A new chime he had tied to the blue spruce rang as a breeze jumped through the garden.

For two summers I did not return, working in Nova Scotia to earn my tuition for the fall. Once I received a card with a rose pressed carefully, the red of a cold winter sunrise: I thought of the garden when grey winds blew in off the iron sea. He sat in it, warm, content, basking in green and yellow and in the love of God. Water ran past his feet and the robins and blackbirds and sparrows thrashed their wings in its coolness.

I came home. Mother and Father's garden was half its size, twelve neat rows of radishes, peas, beans, and lettuce. I did not walk down the lane for several days.

The garden was brown. Poles leaned in all directions. The river of

God was a strip of dried mud. No, there was a spot of colour, a yellow rose drooped, its stalk limp. I opened the gate. It was stiff. Fruit and vegetables had begun in hope and died. He was crouched on the red bricks by ROSA. I hadn't seen him at first. There were grey branches screening him and he himself seemed grey and shifting, like a raw February wind.

"Sir," I greeted him.

"You have been gone a long time." He stood up and forced a smile. His face sprouted sharp black hairs. He shook my hand without strength.

"Do you know your Holy Bible?" he asked me.

"Yes."

"How many gardens are there?"

"I don't know."

"There is Eden. And the garden of Heaven. Yes. And a garden of Love in the Song of Solomon. Father Ferley showed me that. All kinds of gardens. But I didn't realize. I didn't think."

He bent to pick a dried strawberry and roll it between his fingers.

"What about the other? The darkest one? The garden of blood and betrayal? The God who crushes. Did you know that Gethsemane means oil press? So our Lord Jesus prays and there is no way out of life. The doors are shut. All is black. The blood is squeezed out of him. I did not see this garden, just the others, the bright ones. What a fool."

He sat down by ROSA again and looked up at me, his eyes drawing further and further into his skull. "They came with their wives, Carolina with her husband. And the children. My grandchildren. I had never seen the grandchildren. They rented a big van in Toronto and they came together. A great party. They drove out of their lane into a semi truck. That is how all my children die. No. Carolina at least I have left. She cannot move her arms or legs but she can talk. That is good. So this is Gethsemane now. Not Eden."

"I'm sorry. I'm sorry. We can, I can help you. I'll plant it. I'll water it. You won't have to do a thing."

"No!" I had never heard him shout. "It is Gethsemane. Let the thorns grow back and all the plants die. The soil dry up. Let the sun beat on it and make it a desert. It is a garden of death and betrayal. I do not want to see you in the garden again. Water nothing. Plant nothing."

I was home the entire summer but I did not see him again. Like a dying spider, the brown garden curled its vines and stalks and roots up into itself and ceased to move or breathe. Thunder. Lightning. Summer rain. Hail. An arbour collapsed. The fence began to sag. Brown dissolved into black. In September I flew to Hamilton and to seminary.

He sent me a Christmas card. I opened it to a dead, brown, yellow rose and a dozen securely glued thorns and several squashed beetles.

In February there was another card. It was typed. This one was from Carolina. When March break came, I took a plane home.

He would not answer to my knocks. So I walked in. The dishes were clean in the drying rack. The floors shone. The carpet was free of dirt. All the windows took in the spring light. There were baskets of flowers in every room. All the flowers were silk or plastic. But well dusted.

He was watching a game show, withered in a large brown leather chair.

"How is school?" he asked.

"Fine."

"And you learned something from the Holy Bible?"

"Yes."

"What do you learn about death?"

"Come to the garden with me."

"No."

"We can dig it up. Turn it over. Get rid of the thorns."

"No. It is a garden. A special garden."

"It isn't the only garden."

"It is the truest garden."

"No."

"Get out. If I see you in my yard, day or night, I will call the police."

"When did you see Carolina last?"

"She is dead."

"She's at the hospital in Toronto."

"They are all dead."

"You never answer her letters. You never visit."

"Who can visit the dead?"

"You could go to her. Take her hand. Squeeze it. She'd feel that."

"Who can hold a dead daughter's hand?"

I do not know how much he slept each night. If he heard me, he chose not to come out. But perhaps the blustery March wind that scraped and rasped against the walls of his house covered the scrape and rasp of my own tools, my Father's tools. I worked half the night. It was Maundy Thursday. But I did not finish. I returned the next night, Good Friday. It was utterly black, as if the sky had been blinded. I chopped. I dug. Shovelful after shovelful. I came back Saturday night too, clawing up the thorns, hacking at them with my hoe, smacking pick into rock as I had done as a boy. It rained. I worked until a filthy dawn seeped down over my head. I carried my tools home and washed my hands and face and ate a piece of toast. When the morning was silver, I returned.

What would Old Man Reynolds have done if one of us had pitched a rock through his picture window? I took up a large stone and hurled it. The window shattered. He came running to the gaping hole.

"Are you crazy?"

"Come to the garden with me."

"I am calling the police."

"My youngest brother died of a seizure. Before there was any garden. My other brother was killed in a plane crash up north when you turned seventy. I came to the garden when you asked me to. I kept coming to the garden no matter what."

He staggered out of the house in his undershirt and pants and bare feet. Glass had cut one of his toes and blood patched the sidewalk. He came into the backyard and his eyes shot back and forth angrily.

"What is this? Who did this? You did this! You put up a cross! What's that on it? What did you do?"

"It's the gardener."

"What are you talking about?"

"It's God."

"You're crazy."

"He's the gardener. He's on the cross. He's dead. Your Garden of Gesthemane wasn't complete."

"Take it down."

"There's another garden."

"There is no other garden. Take it down."

I swung an axe that had been leaning against the house, weathered and rusted. The steel slammed into the wood. His eyes jumped and he stepped quickly away from me. I chopped ten or twelve times and the cross, cut through, collapsed, along with the effigy, a bearded figure in dark green overalls that rolled over and over until clutched by the thorn bush.

With the cross down he saw the hill of earth I had built up in the corner of the yard. It was wet and ugly, branches and roots jabbing out of it like the fingers of tortured hands.

"What did you do there?" he demanded.

"It's the other garden."

"It is a pile of mud."

He walked towards it. On the other side was a ragged hole. He approached it, his feet slick with mud and water. He dropped to his knees to look in.

"There's nothing," he growled.

"It's a grave."

"What?"

"How well do you know the Holy Bible? You can't find the living among the dead."

His face was streaked with dirt when he looked at me. "You are a sick boy," he said softly. "Go home and do not come back. We were friends once so I will not call the police."

"There was another garden. It had death in it too. It had a grave. And they put God in the grave. Dead. But he wouldn't stay put. And a woman came to see his body and to honour him and to bury God properly. After all, God had done some good, hadn't he, before we murdered him? She couldn't find the body. It broke her heart. She looked around her, crying, and saw flowers and herbs and green bushes. She was in a paradise, a beautiful garden. The air was filled with bees and insects and birds and the smell of morning roses. Then she saw some-one walking in the garden. But no. It was just the gardener, tending the roses, smoothing the ground near the evergreens, pulling up weeds. He looked at her. What are you crying about? he asked her. Who are you looking for? She said, They've taken God away. And I don't know where to look for him. The gardener yanked the gloves off his hands and rubbed his face and came towards her. Mary, he said."

The van was late but it pulled slowly into the lane while I was speaking. An attendant in white came out and slid open the side door and operated a lift. There was the loud hum of machinery. A woman in a wheelchair was lowered to the ground outside the broken gate.

"Papa," the woman said.

119

He stood in the mud and brambles, staring at her, a drizzle from the morning clouds glistening over his head and arms and face.

"Please open the gate for me."

He suddenly moved, pulling at the gate, wrenching it, until she moved her left hand just enough to push the button and send the wheelchair forward into the dirt and stone of the yard. Her lap was full of flowers—roses, daisies, lilies. They were all wrapped carefully at the bottom.

"They have their roots and their soil, Papa," she said. "I've come to plant them. It's Easter Sunday. It's the beginning of the world."

Her father came and knelt by the chair. His back shook and heaved. He put his head into her lap, into her flowers, and she lowered her face and cried against his hair and neck. The soft rain gleamed over everything, over skin and stone and earth and death and white roses.

They planned the new garden together. I simply dug and planted alongside him, doing whatever I was asked. Seeds, transplants, pulling up thorns, watering saplings, piling up stones, levelling mounds, turning the rich black soil. The river of God ran again and instead of St. Francis there was a tall white angel. The pond reappeared. Herbs blossomed pink and white and purple. Flowers of all colours spilled over into the walkways. The arbours were repaired and glittered in red grapes. It was Eden again. It was Heaven.

But in the midst of all the brightness and greenery he left a patch of dry earth and rock and violent thorns and the stump of the cross I had cut down. Just beyond this was a white arbour twisted with white roses. Once through the arbour one found red bricks firmly set, etched ROSA and FRANKY and ANTHONY, along with the names of their wives and children and Carolina's husband. Surrounding this whirl of red were the most amazing flowers in the whole garden, full and rich and brimming over onto the bricks and names. They were all perennials and they rose in whites and crimsons and purples and golds from the blackness of the earth every spring without fail. It is here that he sat, smiling, calling Buon giorno! each morning I passed by, the sun draping his body, Carolina often beside him in her chair. And when the summer rains fell it made their flesh shine like the clearest glass.

So it does not matter that he died or that Carolina left or that the house was sold to another man and his wife who cared nothing for flowers or dwarf cherry trees or the black earth. They cemented it over and built a garage and when I come to visit my widowed Mother now the naked eye sees no Eden, no Gethsemane, no Garden Tomb, no Heaven with the leaves for the healing of the world. But the garden is eternal for I hold it in my soul. And others must too. For one July morning I followed a sound, a most incredible brilliance of sun and light and sky, whirling and rising in a new summer's grace, and I found a meadowlark tightly gripping the edge of the garage roof, calling, crying, casting out her song to the day star again and again, as if she knew what lay under the cold grey slab below and what, one day, must burst forth and break it into pieces.

16

O Holy Night

Others had always complained about Christmas and its commercialization, many preferring the perceived deeper spirituality of the Easter season, but I had never been in agreement with them.

I had no problem, I felt, seeing through all the dazzle and tinsel to the heart of Christmas, and I revelled in the season—cards, wise men, angels, mangers, shepherds, cake, turkey, cranberry, toys and Messiahs all wrapped up in star bright winter nights. So when the opportunity came to travel to Bethlehem over the Christmas season with others from my church I was the first to approach the pastor.

Our pastor was a gaunt man. I signed my name to the sheet and gave him my deposit in cash. He stuck the money in a drawer in his desk.

"You're quite the Jingle Bells," he said. "The trip may disappoint. Perhaps you'd prefer your Christmas here in the snow."

I shook my head. "I've loved Christmas all my life. The crassness of North America has never blunted that. I'll be fine in Bethlehem."

When you are excited about something, long trips mean nothing. The flight touched down in Israel about ten at night and while the pastor had the face of an owl, I was as lively and as talkative as the squirrel that got away. Sleeping at the King David Hotel was a further stimulant, so I did not sleep. The next morning when the bus chugged up to board us for Christmas Eve in Bethlehem, my eyes were red but flashing, darting, taking in everything. I was awake and coiled in my seat while others sagged and slept again.

This was Bethlehem before the Palestinian takeover, before the banners of Christ walking arm-in-arm with Yasser Arafat. As I stepped down into the brittle night air of Manger Square, my way was immediately barred by a gate and by Israeli soldiers with Uzis. All of Manger Square was under patrol. I saw soldiers on the rooftops, snipers, machine guns. I produced a passport, was thoroughly searched, the soldiers stepped aside, I passed through the gate.

Bright lights, bright lights. Masses of people. Our church group could not get into the Church of the Nativity, that had been packed for hours, and the Square itself was jammed with bodies that glittered under the high intensity lights and the strings of white Christmas bulbs. A massive screen had been erected that would allow us to view the Christmas Eve Mass on the outside while it took place on the inside of the church. I wandered, gazed. People pushed against me, struck me, scowled. Shops that rimmed the Square were open for business: pictures of Mary and Joseph, toy sheep, crosses made out of genuine olive wood from the Mount of Olives, Bibles stamped that they had been purchased in Bethlehem, nativity sets hastily carved and even more hastily painted, so that Joseph's eyes bulged in a misshapen face daubed crimson, postcards of Bethlehem with shepherds in first century garb tending their flocks in amber fields under azure skies, racks of Church of the Nativity miniature spoons. I bought nothing. I emerged from a shop to see several of our men rescuing one of our young women from a gang of teenagers who leered and taunted and coaxed for sexual favours. She was crying. Angry, I looked about for police or soldiers. A stage lit up suddenly and various choirs began to perform carols in languages from around the world. The crowd listened. Our church group placed our girls and women within a protective circle and began to listen too. Most of the carols I did not know and could not understand. A paper bag was thrust into my hand—a bottle of Seagram's whiskey. I placed it on the ground and noticed that all about me were people nipping from bottles in brown paper bags, presumably to keep off the chill. Someone had gotten sick and was on their knees, heaving. As I tried to focus on the carols again drunken wailing rose up from behind me. What were they singing? Silent night? I glanced up but the bright lights obliterated any stars.

I plunged my hands deeper into my pockets and hunched my

shoulders against the cold. They never led us in any carol singing, so we were silent as choir after choir sang unknown and exotic pieces. It was midnight. The large screen flickered and flashed and it was the Pope himself, wasn't it, performing the Mass in black and white. He moved silently among the chalices and the candlesticks, the gold and the silver. There was no sound. A fight broke out beside me and almost knocked me down. Fists flailed, the fighters cursed, a bottle smashed and its liquid spread rapidly over the ancient paving stones. People separated the two men, who still attempted to kick each other. More drunken singing from in front—O Little Town of Bethlehem. I began to pace restlessly to warm myself and I came up against my pastor, looking gaunt.

"How are you enjoying Christmas Eve in Bethlehem?" he asked.

I vented. I was disgusted by the drunkenness, I told him. By the gangs of roaming, lecherous youth. Fights. Lights. Pieces of the true manger for sale glued to snow-white cardboard. Soldiers and guns and danger and menace. It was nothing like Christmas, nothing remotely close to the heart of Christmas. It was a disgrace.

The pastor stared at me. "It is Christmas. It is precisely the first Christmas."

The cold deepened. More bottles were passed. On the screen grey and white shadows drifted back and forth. There was more drunken singing, though most people stood silently, staring at the screen. A man reeking of wine passed out against me and fell to the hard, smooth stones. I looked at him. I took my hands from my pockets, knelt and wiped the spittle from the man's face. I tried to wake him up but he would not stir. So I held the stranger's head in my lap. Finally, close to Christ, I worshipped.

17

Good God

Each night the Canada geese come, shouting and honking, and land on the pond, acting as if they were a crowd of noisy tourists pulling off the freeway and into the parking lot of a motel. They flap in over the town from a northeasterly direction and always when the light is almost gone, so that you can barely discern their moving forms. They arrive in clusters of three or six, sometimes a dozen, or even thirty, each group choosing its own portion of water. If I walk to the pond with the dogs in the early morning between six-thirty and seven, just before the sun itself comes to the same place, the geese will still be there.

My dogs dance ahead, into the tall grass, thrust their noses under old timber, hunt vigorously for mice and voles. A few of the geese grumble at their presence but the dogs are not interested in the geese. Every now and then there is a burst of yammering, the geese in one group calling over to the geese in another part of the pond. Some individuals are louder than others, bellowing through their noses, drowning out everyone else. There is a great deal of murmuring within each party, at times something like a good belly laugh rising up into the morning air with the white mist. Wings flap, feathers are examined, the geese drift on the tea-coloured water like great grey ships turning slowly on their anchor cables. Then the sun tops the hills and sprays a fine gold dust over grass, bush, pine, and pond, so that we all, dogs and geese and man, glint and burn like metal. It is when this light arrives, and not before, that the geese begin to leave.

They do not go all at once, they fly cluster by cluster, crying out as they lift themselves over the pond. Some do not leave the water for ten or fifteen minutes after others have taken wing. Eventually they all return to the sky.

They start out heading east then swing sharply back onto the freeway that runs south. The fabric of the day is blue now and they move against this blue. They do not fly in a V-shaped wedge but in a ragtag clump that changes shape often and that has sometimes one goose as the leader, sometimes another, and sometimes no apparent leader at all. They disappear, still conversing loudly, excited perhaps about the warmer sun that awaits them at the end of their long journey. I remain on the ground, among the grasses white-tipped with frost, near to the dark pond with its mallard ducks paddling about and dipping their bills, studiously ignoring the departure as they did the arrival of the geese and their overnight stay. The dogs continue to root among the trunks of fallen poplars. That evening a new crowd of geese will swoop down and splash onto the pond for a night's sleep.

I gaze upon the solemn transition. The first frost comes in the middle of August and kills our tomato plants, our cucumbers, and many of our flowers. But it is an abnormally early frost, one of a kind, and true and consistent frost does not arrive until October. Then I see our carrot patch bent under pale ice crystals each morning. By noon, the green stalks will be as tall and green as summer forest, glistening with the melted frost as if from a fall of rain. You can sit out in short sleeves, the sun shouting almost as brashly as it has during the summer, brown and red working into your skin.

But then it snows ninety minutes up the road at Anahim Lake, and the first fall of snow comes and goes at Kleena Kleene, a half hour's drive. I know our turn is coming. The afternoons are still clear and blue and warm, but only after mornings of cold white haze, dawns where the sun cuts a hole into the world, a brilliant blaze shrouded in thick smoke. There is an edge to the morning air, to the night air, subtle, touching you only if you remain outside twenty minutes or more, but the blade is certainly at work, prying the sun out of the sky.

One Saturday I step from the house and enter a realm of the opaque: white fog, white grass, white and stiff water. Everything is obscured. I go along the gravel lane through an abandoned forestry site. Trees fade and emerge. The land is a ghost. I crunch across the brittle gravel into the past. I am part of a white and grey snapshot from my parents' photograph album and it is 1940 or 1950. I am disembodied. The buildings and the grasses disappear. I am alone in a muffled drum.

It is one of those rare days scattered over the year as a crystal wineglass is shattered over a pallid rug. As the sun arches its neck it does not bring gold but silver. The stars have fallen to the earth in the chill dark and plated the soil in a dull but glossy metal, like the pewter tankard at the house I lift crackling with bright cider. It is a tenuous world, a fragile world, for all its cold strength, a world of shard and fragment.

I wade through the white and the cloud and catch hold of a tree before it drops back. I run a gloved finger swiftly down a branch and powder glitters and swirls up against my face. The limb becomes black where the ice crystals have leaped into space. Soon the entire empire will disintegrate in a similar fashion as the sun, not yet conquered, flames steadily above the intricate and colourless embroidery. Our tender philosophies, our scant mornings of dream.

In a week the land is pearl. I walk my horse down lanes of lodgepole pine, their branches bent under sheaves of white harvest. Occasionally we come upon a clearing where the sun pierces unobstructed and runs a blue needle along the drifts. I pull into myself, with my breath, the clarity and precision of the morning, and I urge the white gelding to a trot, so that my face is gone, cut to slashes of sun and strokes of shadow, the black of the autumn pond. I find an old trail used by deer and hare and coyote and slow to a walk once more, bending my neck to avoid branches and twigs. A squirrel shrieks. A raven pounds its wings at the air. Then it is only the snapping of horse hoof against ice.

My horse I brush down in the stable and leave a black bucket of oats. I return to the house laden with frost and theology. Hot tea and warm soda bread with butter and jam I set on the table. I thank God, I drink, I eat, soon I will sleep. Already the dogs rest in the squares of white light dropping at the windows. Their fur is wet with melted snow. I have an odd, child-like sensation: I have ventured into the silver hall of that most ancient palace. I have kissed the princess. It is all of it a new life. I start a fire in the stove and the heat nicks my fingers and my face. The wood curls yellow. Old years going up and disappearing. I find a book and my chair. I close my eyes. Over me, all over me, the snow, I am covered, I am white and pure and resting, and there is no need to do anything more, not ever again.

18

Wick

Nothing of him that doth fade but doth suffer a sea-change into something rich and strange. So sings Ariel in *The Tempest*. So speaks Shelley's grave, where the lines are etched on his headstone. I carried the words in my own head from English classes and drama clubs. But the words would not stay in my head, they refused. Through heart and soul and marrow they made their way. And they carried me with them.

The change began at a graveyard but I did not know it. Hundreds of headstones. Like white and grey stalks chopped close to the earth. Like a field of stubble. Many of them indecipherable, the inscriptions obscured by rain and wind and the whip of the sea. Every third or fourth grave LOST AT SEA. An hour of raking storm. Clouds sagging into the grass, saltwater scraping and scouring, dark green trees erupting. A battlefield cemetery. An Atlantic Flanders. The drowned fishermen beneath their stones, row on row. Or not under the stones. Their bodies streaming kelp or blossoming with red coral.

At the house all the windows faced the highway. The sea flew blue and ecstatic from the bluff the house was built on, but the entire wall facing it was white and windowless. Clapboard from bottom to top. Unless you opened a door and stepped out, all you could see from inside the house was a brown wall with its cupboards and crockery and a framed print of grass amber and tall in a meadow. The house might have stood in the middle of Saskatchewan or the Dakotas.

The uncle was much shorter than my gangly six foot, glasses, bald, the swell of a paunch, not needing to stoop when he entered through a side door into the kitchen. It was night. He had tied his boat to the dock below the house. Uncle Berwin shook my hand firmly and smiled, the glasses fogging—"You're welcome here, Andrew." He never bothered to remove the glasses, simply washed his hands and sat down at the table while the lenses cleared. He prayed over the food in a voice that was comfortable with giving instructions, even to God. He opened his eyes that first supper and stared at the food, his wife sitting across from him.

"What's all this?" he demanded.

Aunt Hazel, wishing to celebrate my visit, had spread the table with new dishes: fish deep fried and coated with a fancy herbal butter, potatoes sliced up like coins and baked in a cream sauce, raw vegetables whirling in an orange-green-red circle about a bowl of dill-flavoured dip, wedges of Camembert cheese on a cutting board along which crackers were splayed like playing cards.

I chewed with the hunger of the rainy day and its blustery winds. Uncle Berwin ate bits and pieces with the flat eyes of a dead fish. He spooned out as little as possible, so that his plate remained a huge whiteness with daubs of colour. I had almost finished when he laid down his fork and spoke: "Hazel, when I come in to eat, I don't want no surprises."

I had bought a book of sea prose and poetry as a gift for Uncle Berwin. I gave it to him that night as the three of us sat and talked around the wood stove in the front room. He thanked me, flipped through the pages, glancing at black and white photographs of combers and sailboats and gulls. I was excited because I felt I was opening an incredible window into his own world for him. He'd grown up on fishing boats, the swells under his feet, the sky sprawling over his head. Now he could read some of the great writers of the sea, Conrad and Masefield and Hemingway. All the dawns he had been unable to articulate, the storms, the joy of riding out a gale, whitecaps exploding against sky and wind, the mystery of fogs shrouding coves and islets, these would boil up out of his blood and burn through the veins of words and stanzas. The poetry would capture the sea's majesty and power for him, express in haunting tones the sensations his years on the Atlantic must have aroused in him. I spoke and thought like a fool. Uncle Berwin never read the book. It sat under layers of Halifax dailies and bright copies of *Time* and *The Financial Post*. I would dig it out and place it at the top of the pile but it was always smothered once again, never thumbed.

An odd pair to be going handlining for cod together. I with a copy of Conrad's short stories in my lunch bucket, he with his newspapers and nautical charts. I pointing out dawn splendour, he peering at the depth sounder, the glow fastened on his face. Stripping, I might strike into the blue and green waves on a smooth yellow evening. But he didn't know how to swim. Before bed, I would try to write my own poetry about the sea. Uncle Berwin snored in front of the TV.

I had grown up dreaming of breakers and sailing ships and islands. People were confused by this. "You grew up on the prairies, why are you interested in the sea?" The prairies don't have one. Go through the homes of a hundred families in Winnipeg or Calgary or Saskatoon and twenty of them will have posters of sailboats on the walls or framed sea prints or plastic models of square riggers. You hunger for what you never knew. As a boy my imagination had been volcanic with *Treasure Island*, *Robinson Crusoe*, Sir Francis Drake and the Golden Hinde. I went to the shores of Lake Winnipeg and saw the grey rolling ocean. I longed for the day I might place a foot in the Pacific, then later dip that same foot in the Atlantic. Should I keep a jar of water from each? At eighteen I came to Nova Scotia and the graveyard of fishermen in Lunenburg, the clapboard house on the South Shore, Uncle Berwin walking up from his Cape Island boat. And radiating out azure and jade behind all of them, like the spread of a peacock's feathers, the Atlantic.

I had anticipated the furious breakers, the blood gashes of dawn, the reek of salt, the honed wind, the holocaust of cloud and light, and I exulted in all of it. The storms that pinched the good humour from Uncle Berwin's mouth broke mine wide with laughter. When rigging screeched and snapped at metal stays in the blasts of wind, I stood in great peace while he moved restlessly about the boat. Saturday night, a week's fishing behind us, I impulsively grabbed a cousin and spun her about the pier, shouting a sea shanty to the stars and moon. Uncle Berwin came by to check on the boat and smiled at us, unsure, his mouth frozen in an upward jerk of his lips.

The idea had been that I meet the Maritime side of the family, spend the summer working for Uncle Berwin, who needed a hand anyway, fall in love more deeply with the sea, and make some money for university, as I would receive a share of the profits from the fishing. I smelled the water as soon as the Greyhound hissed and opened its doors in downtown Halifax. All around me, in that May dark, were lappings, and gurglings, and what sounded like wet kisses, and strokings, and sighs. The ground did not seem stable or dry. There was a movement, a rocking, a dampness. Lights floated out there, tiny yellow lights on black viscous fluid. I boarded a smaller bus for Lunenburg. Night poured through my open window. It was warm and scented and full of distances.

I stood on the sea as a fisherman at four in the morning, scant hours after the Camembert cheese and the raw vegetables, only a few minutes after hurriedly swallowing bacon and toast and Gravol. Uncle Berwin supplied the Gravol every morning. I was determined to stop using it as soon as I was certain my stomach would not betray me.

It was icy. The stars nicked my eyes. The throb of the engine seemed somewhere else, part of another experience. I skinned my knuckles casting off, my hand movements awkward and jerky, the rope taut as steel and unyielding, but I scarcely noticed, absorbed in our passage across the sea, letting every pitch of the deck move up my leg to my mind, every gleam of light pin itself to my eye, every cold breeze shear my cheek, every breath of wetness, of gasoline, of fish scales and old blood storm into my brain and take utter control. I moved with the ship, my hands in the pockets of my jeans, rigid, unspeaking, flowing in a trance of ultimate sensation and liquid sensuality.

But the sea was harder than a poem, more brutal than Hemingway's blunt, thudding prose. It opened me to the bone. Uncle Berwin would knock on my bedroom door every morning, reaching with his fist into my shoal of sleep and hauling me out half-dead: "Andrew. Time to get up." Three o'clock. I thumped downstairs, too tired to stop my legs from hurling all my body weight into each foot. Aunt Hazel was there in a purple flannel housecoat, eyes puffy, but her dark hair clean and calm. She stirred eggs with a fork, brewed coffee, pinched bread out of the toaster. I drank juice, ate the eggs without ketchup, swallowed the Gravol pill. "Have a good day, Andrew," she smiled, patting me on the shoulders. Early that summer, in all those dark mornings, I saw she was beautiful, as lovely as the warmth and security of sleep, as strong and splendid as the red and black sunrise. But once through the door stars stabbed, cold gnawed, fingers were shaved by hemp that rasped down my hands like a bastard file. The engine thumping into your body. Lines dropping over the side, dawn at the shoulder a welt, the yellow of a bruise, hauling up, tossing the cod into a box, rebaiting the hook, grabbing for another line, and tugging. Ten minutes for lunch. Sandwiches, a thermos, some fruit, candies, peanuts, blessed Aunt Hazel, as if we were opening a Christmas stocking. More of the hauling, the baiting, the tossing, the thick slapping of tails, like a kid flicking a garden hose. Rain or shine. Water striding along neck and spine or sun cooking your cheek and ear. Sometimes a breeze of talk, sometimes nothing. Your mind empty most of the day, maybe images from a TV show, usually the most irritating ones, or of a girl's strong face. The rest of the time sea waves, surging blue steel, exuding cold at your face and hands as if it were a wind instead of an ocean. Back again, the sun low, almost lost, the planet rinsed in gold, a sonnet in every wave, but after the cleaning, the blood and slime, the fish heads and iron eyes, the whole mess cast into the water at the dock, the filets packed in salt like shovelfuls of snow, Aunt Hazel's soup and beef and bread, no strength in the fingers to hold a pen, no flat calm in the head for words to flow out of, only a spinning of flotsam, standing to wash your hands and the room dipping from one side to the other, the sensations you were oblivious to all day rising like swells to dominate your consciousness, forcing you to adjust to the pitch of a deck as you stood on the kitchen floor, splash and towel your face because it is burning off, stare at the TV and see lines running from your hands, or the ghost images of the depth sounder, dream of rattling water, fish jaws closing and opening, blue sky yawing into blue fields of ocean and the bright snapdragons of whitecaps.

But the cold, even on the hottest days, the waves chopping into your arms as you lean over the hull, the gouging of the wind, your pants soaked, your shirt splashed, your socks curled up in your boots, rain crackling onto your head, light scrabbling over it, chill one moment, scorching the next, as if you had the flu. Often the sun seared you in such a way that you felt cold from the burn, not heat. And to the cold, the weeks piled on the drudgery of the routine, the exhaustion of going to bed at eleven and getting up at three, the sense of isolation from the rest of the earth in a summer that consisted only of fishing, eating, and sleeping.

By the middle of June I did not see the early stars and I did not lift my head to scan the east for that thumbnail of light. Blue became as monotonous, as encircling, as entrapping as grey, and the mighty globe-straddling wind, that sighing, roaring thing that could set the sea ablaze in a white heat for a thousand miles, it became chisel and hammer, no more. The *Cape Islander* moving out into the open again Monday morning, my head aching for more sleep, my whole body screeching for more warmth, the water peeling back pale on either side of us, I stared back at the yellow drops that were the lights of the house and realized the sea had become a tedious chore and that I had come to loathe it.

But it was impossible to curse. Uncle Berwin, at fifty-five, took sharp sun on his face and arms, hooks in his fingers, cruel wind chopped at the back of his neck. Still he steered the *Cape Islander* into the exploding Atlantic, found the cod, baited a dozen lines and jerked them up one after the other and rebaited them, his glasses flecked as if with spit, his fingers, large and round and brown as cooked sausages, pushing chunks of squid onto the barbs. At home he seemed no more than a retired teacher, drooping over his paper in a well-stuffed armchair, his glasses sliding down the bridge of his nose. On the water, I did not notice his baldness or his paunch or his mild round face. I saw a fisherman performing one task on top of another, his lips flat and still, hands jumping like the strong wings of a Bonaparte gull. Steel was all through the man, working itself out against careening wind and tumbling sea. I felt I must stay beside him, fumbling with hook and line, ripping the iron through bleeding mouths. Like him, straddling a few planks of wood on a leaping ocean, I must endure.

Each day became a load to be borne with objects digging into your back as you heaved the whole mess onto your shoulder. To gain strength, I closed off every extra room in the house of my mind. I focused on fighting the cold, jerking up the lines, splitting the cod. I ate and watched TV no matter what was on. Glossy Penguin paperbacks, chosen for their artistic covers, famous authors, and profound subjects, remained stacked on my bedside table. No creases grew along their spines. I only had enough in me to survive the bludgeoning of the sea.

Sunday was different, alone of all the days. I had no use for churches and boisterous ministers, but I made up my mind not to offend my uncle or my aunt. Just before eleven in the morning I walked with them along a gravel road to a white clapboard Baptist church with a solid square steeple like the turret on a fort. We sat still as rock. Hymns with old English words were sung at precisely timed moments, men in dark navy suits passed gleaming plates along each straight pew, the Bible was read in monotone, the minister rose in a black robe. His voice was firm and quiet, like sea and shore on a sultry day, and it carried with it that same sort of hypnotic rhythm. I listened to him every week despite my intention to daydream. His head seemed small and clownish emerging from such a voluminous robe and the steel-rimmed rectangular glasses on his white face added to the sense that he was out of his element—many of the scarlet and orange necks, cracked with fissures, belonged to men I'd seen on the open water. But the minister continued to speak in his steady manner and they continued to sit and I came away every Sunday with the sense of having indulged in a dry, overcooked, but substantial roast beef dinner. I grew to like the solid order of the service, the measured beat of its predictability, the sturdy plainness, and I counted on the stability it offered me as much as I counted on Aunt Hazel's meals—the Camembert never returned—and the luxury of being able to sleep in until nine each Sunday morning. I wanted reliable pleasures, things I could trust to make me feel sane and happy. A steady, uninterrupted flow of normality. If for some reason the usual Sunday pattern was disturbed, or those few precious hours after fishing each evening were scattered, I felt a toppling inside my brain, a loss of balance, and it was difficult to prepare myself to grip the heaving, tossing sea the next morning. I would become depressed, sit grimly over my eggs at breakfast, slump like fog as the boat headed out.

Sleep was no help in the battle. Waves continued to erupt like massive dark towers into my dreams, looming over my head and over the boat. Cod slapped themselves into lifelessness. Their bloody entrails drifted down to where the pilings of the dock drove down into the muck. Lines sawed into my palms. The horizon swung one way and then the other as swells rolled their backs up under the keel of the boat. Uncle Berwin's knock came like a gunshot, something I was never prepared for, and I clambered awkwardly out of the black deep and into the other, lightless under the light of a hundred thousand stars.

I began to think of the cemetery in Lunenburg, of the men never buried there, no skeletons under the stones that bent chiselled with their names, their skulls leering out of splintered timbers bristling with barnacles and weed, down under my feet, hundreds of them, mile after mile, as we rumbled into the peeling night. The cod had eaten their limbs and hearts and passed on the stuff of this scavenger's feast in their spawning. At the house I was certain my thoughts were nonsense, but in the cool, groping hours of dawn, leaning over the dark, churning water, I became confused and apprehensive.

One afternoon Uncle Berwin came alongside another *Cape Islander*. He knew the two men and they called back and forth a few minutes. The one in green overalls and a New York Mets cap tossed some pollock over to us for bait. We pulled away and left them to their fishing ground. Uncle Berwin was at the wheel and I was standing behind him. He jerked his head.

"The man with a baseball cap. He's had a hard go. He comes in from a day's fishing two year back. Supper'll be ready in another ten minutes, his wife says. So he goes to his shed to look over some of his gear. She takes a bread knife and pulls it across her throat. I don't know where she got the strength. She might as well have cut his throat too and be done with it."

The acres and acres of sea that sprouted only fog and wind and damp. Her entire life it had caged her in, her husband a fisherman, until she smuggled defiance into her cell and lifted the knife. I cried in the bathroom, running the tap so neither of them could hear. I'm sorry, I kept saying to this dead woman, I'm sorry, I'm sorry. For the silver-crested poems and my long hours of worship, creamy foam curling at my feet, while I stood in a prairie field under a rising wind. The minister with the quiet voice had buried her. With his steady, conventional words, not a shred of magic in any of his sentences, he had the stamina to do it. I crumpled the few poems I had written. I scarcely glanced at sunrises or sunsets over the water though Aunt Hazel often tried to draw my attention to them. I stayed in the house and was grateful it was impossible to glimpse the spreading expanse, the blue-eyed killer. I went to bed as early as possible and tried to concentrate enormous amounts of strength there in the dark. I pulled it up by the fistful from somewhere inside. Perhaps there was a God. I was going to survive. I would not be taken.

But my loathing degenerated into fear. A whiteness when I thought of the sea wind uprooting the green trees that shaded drowned men's graves. A panic that yanked me awake and forced me to bang open the window in my bedroom and swallow air rapidly. The only refuge was the routine, the food, Sundays, the words of God, the bank of light we three sat in, the electric lamp burning, as Aunt Hazel sewed and Uncle Berwin slept in his chair. The days writhed around me and tightened, but I could draw in Uncle Berwin's blandness and Aunt Hazel's beauty like strong, hot drink. And there came the night I pulled an old Bible from a shelf, full of envelopes and pressed flowers, and listened for God in the pages. So I withstood the disintegration of my romance.

The seas of August rose up like granite walls and smashed into our boat. In his yellow slicks, Uncle Berwin pulled up cod, flipped them into the wooden boxes, glanced at the depth sounder, threw me some bait, yanked at another taut line. The sun had coloured his face like a ripe pear. When he talked to me his eyes were obscured behind misted lenses and splotches of water. Yet he spoke more often when we were at the house. He even began to tell me jokes, and he laughed, like a burst of hammering on a steel pipe. When we were slashing off the heads of broccoli and cabbage one evening in the garden, he grunted: "You see how she reaches down into your guts like some godawful hand and yanks up whatever she can get ahold of." But back at sea he said very little. He asked a few questions, scarcely responded to my answers, moved constantly back and forth. He became a backdrop, like the regular throbbing of the engine, the thrust of the swells, the swoop and shriek of the gulls. I was distinct, set apart and isolated from sky and sea and boat and Uncle Berwin and the troughs of dying cod, only the charcoal needles of rain and storm impinging on my solitude while they smudged out the horizon and made all things the same.

I kept at my work, almost savage with energy. The fishing itself seemed to pour strength into me. It was a way of resisting. I moved with greater sturdiness and power than I had in May or June or July. I willed my imagination to cease and the handline and its thrashing victim became heaven and earth. I thought I began to pray. And it was in the middle of this flow of intensity I hauled up one afternoon and my arms seemed detached, part of the stone waves that nicked them, the crisp sweating line, the cod with its throat full of sharp iron. My legs and feet, planted on the deck, were one with the roll of the waters, obeying that rhythm. It was living and breathing around me, wet, whirling, gushing, hurtling, beating, groaning.

Sunlight flared like the thin blade of a filleting knife and laid open a dense clot of cumulus, slitting my sight. A surge upward, a dip, a descending. The crests of the waves, flicked with clarity, rushed on with me and the world was bright as nickel and in a great hurry of beauty. The ocean budded and blossomed as if it were an immense leafy oak and, as the gap in the clouds widened and the light spread, the whitecaps littered the sea like thousands of petals. The water shed from my fingers like sparks and the summer ended on a cry.

Waves still pounced at the boat, clouds dropped onto the Atlantic like sticky clumps of clay, the wind bit and scratched, but layer after layer sloughed off me, I felt exposed to air and light and vast distances of water, the sensation I had as a boy when I rose up from the cold of my baptism, streaming from hair and head and arms, and gazed at the people in the church as if they or I had suddenly come into existence. There was an avalanche of saltwater teeming with strength but void of sexuality and intellect and malevolence. Uncle Berwin struck my door. I dressed swiftly and thudded down into the kitchen. On the porch, I pulled the stars into my chest with deep breaths and their sharp, icy points pricked my lungs.

"What's got into you?" asked Uncle Berwin as we were cleaning cod just before Labour Day. "You're soon on your way, is that it?"

I shrugged. "I don't know. I guess I believe in God."

Uncle Berwin stared at me. "This is something new, boy?"

"This kind of God? Yes."

"What kind of God?"

"A God who isn't a monster I have to appease." With a stroke I slit open a final fish. There was the copper blood. There was the silver blade.

I stood in front of the old bureau in the hallway, one with a wooden frame within which the mirror, shaped like an hourglass, swung loosely. A vein had grown high up on my arm over a muscle. Aunt Hazel was as dark and natural as soil. Uncle Berwin appeared as sharp as a splinter.

The grey monotony of the sea had ground down all my edges, even the keen blade of fear and the glimmering thrust of illusion. The perpetual rhythm of the ocean and the eternal beat of the fisherman that matched it exhausted all my foes and dragged me through to the other side. I did not see, my soul nicked by brand new September mornings, that the monotony which had saved me in its killing splendour could as easily pierce the bones of another. Instead of birth, waves and their roaring and the shoals of darkness.

"Put in a window," I teased the night before I left. "You'd like a window, wouldn't you, Aunt Hazel?"

Uncle Berwin did not smile or take his eyes from his newspaper. "The wall is as it is. You're a free man now and you see it another way. But I'm staying and you're leaving."

"If I could stay I'd still want it up. I'd help you. We could fill the whole house with light."

"We got plenty of light. We don't need any of that other. You're quick to forget."

"It's just an ocean, Uncle Berwin. Just water."

"You come out for the summer from where? And you'll tell me what it is? I grew up here. I stood by enough caskets. What's in the sink is water."

"It's not alive. It's not a god."

He put down his paper. "You learned nothing. You lost all you should of kept. Now you're going back with your head full of the same foolishness you brought with you. A brain stuffed with poems. What you're good for is staying there on the prairies. You'd sure die if you stayed out here."

"Uncle Berwin."

"You're completely useless."

"Don't you want a window, Aunt Hazel?"

Uncle Berwin got to his feet. "Shut up, boy."

Aunt Hazel puckered her lips and her eyes were black and narrow as thread. I shrugged, swallowed, and walked upstairs to my bedroom. The TV blasted suddenly through the house. Outside my window the round September moon had risen. It burned in the dark water like a candle wick.

19

The Prophet of Kitsilano

The coyotes are hunting on the hill just behind the house now. When we came to Tatla Lake in the late spring they howled and yipped from across the dirt road, beyond the pond and beyond our nearest neighbours, a quarter mile away. In the summer we heard them when the sun burst the land's hold, and we heard them under the white fire of the night sun. My wife felt that they were only a few feet away when they woke her once at four in the morning, calling. Now they cry back and forth from the forested hill that slopes up from our backyard. And the song has changed. It is not the howl or the hunting bark that rises a tone and asks a question, hanging in the air between wilderness and tentative civilization. It has become a high, thin wail, but a wail full of music like the other songs were not, a harmony from many throats, flinging colour into the pale frosts and opaque dawns. The dogs stop looking for mice and listen and whine and yip and charge about in the mist. Whatever summer or early autumn may have led us to believe, we must now face the truth of it. The wilderness is coming back to claim what is its own, the land where the ranches are built, the forests where the timber is cut, the lakes and rivers where the fish are hunted and killed. The herds we have domesticated it will cull, the animals we have tamed it will inflame, the delicate crops we have cultivated and set out in rectangular rows it will destroy.

✻

I had not thought about any of it until I'd had coffee and cake with Joshua just before my wife and I left Vancouver for the north. It was at a small cafe in Kitsilano. In 1987, Kitsilano was a magical circus of hippies old and new, right wing yuppies with elaborately honed bodies, people of the sea who wandered the beaches or who sailed dinghies or yachts, artists, philosophers, New Agers, tea-cup readers, and a final and generous seeding of individuals bent on a newer world where every supper would be a vegetarian dish and every conversation a well-articulated expostulation of self-discovery, liberation, the essential unity of all faiths, organic gardening, and assorted primal screams. Kitsilano also had old houses and not a few recluses and end-of-the-present-age prophets. Joshua was one of these. He did not have the long forehead for it but he did have the stoop. He was bent over his coffee mug now, long blonde hair separated into two large and untidy heaps, like fistfuls of straw. His glasses were round and had been repaired with white tape at one hinge. His legs dangled under his body, even when he walked, as if they were boneless. Wrists and hands and fingers poked out of the sleeves of a green army jacket, a purple and red-checked flannel shirt, a thin maroon sweater with a V-neck, and an Arrow dress shirt with brown pin stripes. Underneath it all was a white Stanfield cotton T-shirt which could be discerned at his throat. His face was caving in toward his chin which was sharp as the tip of a graphite pencil and sprouted blonde hairs like small slivers of wood. His fingers on the coffee mug were long and white with blue veins and his eyes were the same colour as the veins, gaping out from behind his glasses like two separate and translucent heads stretching out of a cave and blinking at the light. He looked like a lot of other Kitsilano natives who roamed up and down the Greek section of Broadway and wound up browsing through shelves of Carl Jung in the various New Age bookstores, exuding petula oil.

"You look like something that washed up dead on Jericho Beach," I decided out loud.

Joshua shot me a mournful look before peering back at the heaps of white sugar cascading into his coffee from the torn packages between his fingers. The packages sparkled with photographs of deer and beaver and bald eagles.

"There's nothing to joke about," he said. "If you'd seen what I've been seeing you wouldn't sleep or eat either."

I let another jest pause on my lips. At seminary, Joshua had been baby-faced, pudgy, moustached, wore tinted glasses with square frames, blue blazers, navy ties, grey pants, gleaming black shoes. He had smiled at many things and would laugh incredibly loudly. Now he wore old hiking boots, black from coatings of Sno-seal, and his mouth held a line like a ruler while he stirred his coffee with a spoon. I waited, but it became clear that he would say nothing more until prompted.

"Okay, Joshua," I told him. "I'm sorry. Tell me what's been going on."

He lifted the mug to his lips, obscuring most of his face. After a series of short sips he set it down, clutching it in both hands as if it might jump away at any moment. He looked out the window. The sky was grey, the people walking past or waiting at a nearby bus stop evidently fashioned from the same lustreless material.

"It is coming to an end," Joshua finally mumbled.

"What is?"

"This. Us." He looked toward me again, eyes wide, face drooping, as if he might cry, but Joshua never did cry in my presence. "The wilderness is coming back."

"What?"

"Snow in Florida in the summer. The water tables dropping in central BC and the land going back to desert. The water table is dropping under Albuquerque, New Mexico too. The polar ice cap melting and the ocean level rising. We've had our chance and now Nature is moving against us, trying to destroy us before we destroy it."

"Is that all? The Greenhouse Effect, is that it? Too many spray cans, too many cars, the Amazon getting flattened for cattle ranchers?"

"No. All of that's just part of something much bigger. It's the animals. They're coming back to the places that used to be theirs, the places where we've built our cities and our towns and our farms. They know something. They've crossed over the barrier between wilderness and civilization. They're back. They're expecting something."

He drank from his coffee, taking longer, slower sips. Then he set it down and pushed it aside, lacing his fingers under his sharp nose and propping his elbows on the table. He gazed at the small bowl of sugar packages, at the colour photograph of a wolf.

"You've heard about the coyote pack in the forest by the university?" he asked me.

"Yes, as a matter of fact, I have. But no one's seen the pack in years."

"I saw them. Last week. There were six of them. A bunch of others walking their dogs saw them too."

"So?"

"Coyotes. In the middle of the third largest city in the country. What are they doing there?"

"Living and dying and obviously breeding, Joshua. The university has hundreds of acres of endowment land, all of it rain forest."

"They weren't there five years ago."

"I see. They are part of this movement to reclaim civilization for the wilderness, are they?"

Joshua did not look up from his sugar bowl. But he went on.

"They're coming back into Nova Scotia, did you know that? Thousands of them. Hunting in the farm fields and apple orchards. They haven't been seen in any great numbers in Nova Scotia for over a hundred years. And it's not only the coyotes. The whales are coming back. Coming closer inshore. All kinds. As if they have nothing to fear."

"And so they don't, Joshua. The whales are protected now and hunting from other countries is petering out pretty quickly."

"The whales are coming back regardless."

"Look. Coyotes have always been masters at survival and at adaptation. And the decrease in whale hunting has meant an annual increase in the overall whale population."

"Grizzlies are being sighted in parts of the U.S. that haven't seen grizzlies in years," Joshua interrupted me.

"Conservation efforts, " I argued.

"There are only supposed to be five hundred grizzlies left in the U.S. But there are more."

"You've been counting?"

"There are more attacks. More fatalities."

"More people crowding into more places where they shouldn't be."

"One of the last frontiers is the Chilcotin, west of Williams Lake, up where you are going. There's one highway that crawls over that plateau on its way to Bella Coola. It's still half gravel. It's a country of ranchers and trappers and government employees. I was up there this past summer. The water tables are dropping fast. They're getting less snow and less rain. The lakes are shrinking. In a few years the rattle-snakes will be moving west from the Fraser Canyon. A friend of mine killed a rattler near his cabin in the East Chilcotin a year ago. Thick around as your arm."

"Our climate operates in cycles, Joshua. The Chilcotin may become more arid for forty or fifty years, but then the rains and snows will get heavier again and the water tables will rise."

"If you go off the main gravel highway near a place called Tatla Lake, you'll come to a dirt road that winds through a region called West Branch. Fifty or sixty people live down there, most of them in log houses, some with the bark still on. There's no electricity. A few people have diesel generators. The further down the road you drive, the larger the trees get. You're moving into a region of greater moisture, right in amongst the Coastal Mountains. The highest mountains in BC. Glacier after glacier. Where the road stops somebody tried to build a ranch. Wild country. I've been up to the Stikine and Skeena countries, up by Spatzizi and over on up to Alaska and the Yukon and the western Arctic. No place is wilder than that rain forest that starts up where the road through West Branch comes to an end. It's like hiking into green fire. Everything shooting up around you as if the whole forest is desperate. Animals all over the land, behind every rock. Grizzly and cougar and timber wolf. I had to carry a rifle. A big rifle. I used to walk along this creek and fire shots into the air everytime I saw a bush shake. Do you know what that place made me think of? A last line of defence. A place for regrouping. A site for gathering forces together to resist the enemy and then counterattacking against him. The ranch at the end of the road was put up in the fifties. They got that much of it up all right. Then they tried to spread out a bit more. Everyone of those new cabins has been abandoned within the past five years. The snows were so heavy one year the timber wolves came looking. Ate the family dogs and went after the horses. The ranch got snowed it, the snowmobile broke down, the father gets into town on skis. People talked to him at the store in Tatla Lake. But he never went back to his wife and children. Took the bus out to Williams Lake. No one ever heard from him. His family was stuck in one of the new cabins another three weeks.

Finally they got out and they abandoned the ranch. I saw it. The new buildings were five years old and looked a hundred. Wind and snow broke in every window and crushed the roofs. The old homestead itself was full of wolf scat. A pack uses the place as a den. They even use the beds."

"Every generation has its pioneers. They gain some ground and they lose some. Read the literature from a hundred years ago, Joshua. It will sound familiar. You're not describing anything new or unique."

Joshua shook his head. "That's a choice you're making. You can't begin to explain all the vicious weather patterns we have on our hands now, let alone the aggression of the animals and all of Nature. Rationalize all you wish. Thumb through your history books. It explains nothing. Don't you ever feel as if there is a circle around us? That the wilderness is not gone? That something is out there in the dark?"

I did not respond. Joshua played with one of the sugar packages.

"The other cabins were ransacked by grizzlies," he continued. "Grizzlies are the most independent creatures on earth. They have their own territories staked out and they battle any other bear that intrudes. But that family had sold one of the cabins and some land to a loner. And he claims it was three grizzlies working together that kept on harassing him. He saw them twice, always together, adult bears. They tore up his garden, killed what livestock he had, broke down his fences, and finally came after him. He swears they smashed down the cabin door and he jumped out a window and never stopped running. I saw that cabin too. The logs slashed. The furniture in bits and pieces. And the bears had a plan because they went after all the ranches on West Branch. Killing calves. Taking a couple every few weeks. Steers. A bull. One fellow and his hired hand waited out by one of the kills, sitting in the cab of a 4X4 at night. A young bear came out of the bush at dawn and started eating some more of the cow carcass. They shot him from the cab, then they walked over to take a look. Two grizzlies had been waiting. They came charging out of the bush and tore into them. The rancher was killed and the hired hand lost an eye and an arm. He laid there after the bears had mauled him and eventually crawled back to the truck. The rancher's wife picked up and left. Another couple bought the place and a year ago a forest fire burned them out. A huge lightning storm in the mountains. The place is for sale now. As a matter of fact, there's a fair bit of land for sale on West Branch. Going fairly cheap too.

148

Lake front. Mountain views. Acreage. Along with the land comes the wildlife though. The cougars have been making their presence felt lately. Screaming in the night all around the houses. A child was dragged off into the brush by one this past summer. They didn't find anything when they went looking. Not a body, not a scrap of clothing."

"Okay, Joshua. I've had my fill of these true-to-life wild animal stories. All you're describing is the kind of stuff that's gone on from the dawn of time. And you think that it's signalling the end of the world."

"Everyone interprets the facts as they wish. But only one interpretation can be true."

"You think Nature is moving against us. The animals are going to make a series of concentrated attacks over the next few years, is that it? First West Branch, then Vancouver, then the world, right? " I pushed a laugh out of my throat.

"No. That rainforest in from Knighte Inlet and Bute Inlet, and that land all around Mount Waddington—that entire region is a peculiar place. I don't think the animals are coming to wipe us out. I think they're moving into position to take over after we're all gone. Apparently, that is something that is going to take place in the not too distant future. They're moving back into what was once their land and they're waiting. It's just, isn't it? We talk so much about land claims, the claims of the first nations, the white man's claims. We've forgotten who has been here all along, before any human. Weren't they created first? It's their land. Soon God will give it back to them."

"God?"

"Who else signals Nature about what is to come to pass? Who else triggers that instinct of return in the coyote and the timber wolf and the grizzly? "

"So what is it going to be? Another flood? A nuclear holocaust? Another ice age?"

"I don't know. I don't think the animals know either. They only know it will be theirs again. They will have the land to themselves. The wilderness will claim the high rises and the universities and the cathedrals. Are my theories so strange?"

"They have no bearing in reality, Josh."

"But the other end time scenarios do? Geodisic domes to survive under in the deserts? Colonies on the moon and on Mars? Endless population growth fed by endless supplies of synthetic food manufactured by Dupont? Or perhaps I should turn for answers to the Christian community. Our bookstores are stockpiles of plausible end-of-the-world scenarios, aren't they? Every twelve months the Christian publishing houses pump out hundreds of fresh titles. The Antichrist of 1990 will be replaced by the Antichrist of 1991 and 1999. They will tell us to invest in gold or in land. They will tell us to store filtered water and Lipton's soup. We are the last generation. Our economies will fail. Russia will rise up again. China will rise up. The Pacific Rim will rise up. Christ is coming tomorrow night. No, buy my new book, I've changed my mind, Christ comes tonight. Look, look, the North American Christians may actually suffer for their faith—they'll have to sell their second car and third cars and their condos! It really must be the end! Christ truly must be coming soon to deliver us! A billion dollar industry that will burgeon until the end of time. The end of the world industry. Now that really would be something to profitably invest in. No. I think my scenario bears up pretty well compared to the other theories out there that Christians are eager and willing to spend fortunes on and split churches over. What do you think? Do you honestly feel we've put an end to the wilderness? Do you really believe that what is wild and fallen is over and finished? Don't you ever sense its threat? Don't you ever fear that it might break down the barriers and swarm over us?"

Joshua stood up suddenly, banging his knees against the table and sloshing cold coffee onto my hand.

"I've got to get going," he said. "Thanks for the coffee."

I walked outside with him, shook that small portion of his hand he offered me, then watched him move off down the sidewalk. He went at a pace and posture that I can only describe as a lope. For a few moments he had swelled into a lion and his beliefs had taken on fresh logic and strength. I had the strongest feeling about eyes as I stood there on the sidewalk, people brushing past me. I glanced at a small park of trees and clipped grass across the street. This sensation of eyes seemed to be coming from there. I went to the crosswalk, waited for the light, strided over. I knew it was nonsense but my imagination was leaping all over the place and I had to put it to rest. I went over every inch of that park and it took me the better part of thirty minutes. I scanned every hedge, glanced behind every bush and tree, examined the grass for signs of spoor, until the sky darkened and the blade of winter snicked up under my coat sleeve with a gust of wind. It slew several green leaves and flung them across my vision.

There was nothing there, of course.

20

White Man's God

In June the cottonwoods release their seed and for weeks it is a summer's winter. White swirls in and out, tumbling and turning, as if the world is a glass globe a child has lifted and shaken. Overhead, the blue dome is spotted. Some detest the whitefall. I feel it is a time of magic. Anything might step out of the whirling. Anyone might come in out of the storm. And so it is that Jimmy Strikes With A Gun comes my way. June is a new earth in the foothills of the Rocky Mountains.

The town has lived more than a hundred years along the banks of a gold and green creek. Hills rise all around, and in the west, mountains blue, mountains purple, mountains at morning and at dusk. A footpath of gravel edges the banks of the creek. I see him coming, his face like a chisel, a straw cowboy hat tight on dark braided hair. I sense us riding toward each other, a harsh riding, his face cold and blunt, mine sharp and steep and far, rifles in our fists, the plains cracking with the fast hooves of our ponies. But out of the white falling, it is him.

"Jimmy!"

He stares. "White Man's God!" he laughs.

It is March. The city is melting. Water pools in the gutters and glitters in the empty fields. A warm south wind. Parkas are shorn. A smiling. A straightening of backs. The prairie winter is done. Sprinklers are spitting and hissing on the fairways. I am studying journalism, hopelessly behind in my assignments, slumped at a typewriter, trying to work something onto the sheet of paper directly from my head, without a rough draft, the way the pros do it. Tim, round glasses and short beard and jeans, he snips into the room. I lift my head. Soon I am in a car, an LTD, a dark one. There are six of us. Driving down the plains, north to south, from farms to ranches, flat land to hills, greater heat, longer suns, brown grass.

At the last of the fifteen hour drive I am behind the wheel. We have come through night and morning and now it is past noon. Hill after hill. Buffalo—we are not only going south but going into time, it is not only another country but another era. We see a few pickups. Then, for a hundred miles, nothing.

I am still at the wheel when the man swings the machine gun and aims it at my head, the head of the driver, as a man with a gun is trained to do. He is in cavalry blue. But he is no older than I am, standing up in his dirt green armoured car. We are the same. But we started in different places. I brake quickly. The LTD swerves and slithers. I throw up my hands.

"What are you doing?" shout my friends and fellow students. Get going, get going!"

"I've got a gun pointed at my head."

"He's not going to shoot. Get going, get going."

He never relaxes the grip on the gun. The gun is mounted on a swivel and it tracks us. We drive down into the valley at our own risk, he says. We're laughing too much, almost giddy. Both sides have agreed to a temporary truce. The other students back home swore we'd never get in. We tie a pillowcase to our aerial. I'm driving again. Into the valley. Into Wounded Knee.

A raw wind had been blowing at the border between Manitoba and North Dakota. We said nothing about the uprising at Wounded Knee in South Dakota. We stopped for coffee at a local watering hole south of Fargo. Ranchers with curled and battered stetsons. It was 1973—they didn't like the look of my hair. They said something, steam flickering over their hands, clutching their coffee mugs for warmth. I was polite—tired but full of the good will sparkle which comes with impending adventure.

"Pardon me?" I asked.

The ranchers eyed me, then smiled with the blue cut of the ice dawn snagging the windows of the diner: "You got hair like a sheep, boy. We ought to shear you."

The ranchers laughed. I laughed, but from my nose, pretending. I laughed that laugh again when the muzzle of an AK-47 dangled lazily at my stomach.

"Hey. I'm gonna use this white guy as a shield and start blasting."

They were mostly Sioux. They had about as deep and healthy a laugh at my expense as the ranchers had had over ther Saturday morning breakfast. I was standing in the valley with a ridiculous notepad in my hand and there were loaded guns all around me and buildings full of bullet holes and underneath the grass was blood.

The United States government had cut off power to the Knee but someone had jury-rigged a system so the Sioux could still pump up gas from the underground storage tanks. Cars and trucks darted back and forth as we headed toward the station, edging our way down and in from the valley's rim. A car jumped out of the trees and cut us off. They wanted to know how many soldiers and federal marshals were up on top. We drove to the gas station. That's where Jimmy sat, rolling a cigarette. He watched us and listened to us for a few minutes.

"Where's your college?" he asked suddenly.

"Manitoba."

"The Canadian Indians are jerked around worse than we are. And they don't even know it."

A young man with long dark hair, headband, and black-rimmed glasses rode up on a paint, holding the reins to a horse trotting behind him. He held a Winchester lever-action.

"Patrols," said Jimmy.

"Are you all Sioux?" I asked.

"Nah. Cheyenne. Crow. Nez Perce. I'm Blackfoot. Hey. You should have seen the firefight last night. Tracers slamming into everything. Now we got this truce. But it won't last. What are they going to do? Give us back Mount Rushmore?"

The more we relaxed, the more our group split up and wandered, photographing, listening. The South Dakota sun was warm but the breeze held the memory of the dead snow. We slipped on our jean jackets. I stared at bunkers that had been cut into the earth, concrete blocks stacked around their edges. The Catholic church flew the stars and stripes upside down over its doorway. Inside the altar was crammed with a stereo system. Some women were ladling out cups of hot soup. Covers from Dee Brown's paperback, Bury My Heart At Wounded Knee, were taped up in various buildings. Or pieces of foolscap:

WE ONLY DIE ONCE, LET'S ALL DIE HERE TOGETHER

IT'S BETTER TO DIE ON YOUR FEET THAN TO LIVE ON
YOUR KNEES

WOUNDED KNEE (AGAIN)

I was watching them slaughter a steer a native rancher had brought up in the back of his truck. The sun dropped gunmetal blue behind the church. Jimmy walked up with his AK-47.

"Sitting Bull. He was killed just north of here. On the Grand River. Did you know that?"

I shook my head. "Soldiers?"

Jimmy laughed. "Sioux. Indian police. Right after that the soldiers moved up the Grand River Valley into Wounded Knee and opened up with their hardware. Right here. Shot down everybody. Same old story. Women and children. They were afraid of the Ghost Dance. Afraid there'd be another Indian uprising. They were after Spotted Elk. He rode with Sitting Bull. It was Custer's old regiment did the job. The Seventh Cavalry."

The church's steeple was a cross. Two perfect black lines against the blue sunset. Jimmy eyed it.

"You a Christian?" he asked.

I shrugged.

"Methodist?" he prodded.

"Baptist."

"It doesn't make any difference to us. It's all the White Man's God. What do Christians care about freedom and creation and respect? Where are you spending the night?"

"I guess we'll huddle up in the car."

"Better come with me. In case there's shooting."

It was a shack with three or four others sleeping on the floor. I didn't belong. But no one asked Jimmy why. And no one offered me a blanket. I draped my denim jacket over my back and shoulders. Runners for a pillow. It was dark. And cold. But no gunfire.

"Where are the other white kids?"

1970. A high school play on Louis Riel. All the Metis and Cree parts were being played by Metis and Cree. I'd wanted to play Gabriel Dumont. But I wasn't Metis. A tall Cree girl asked me where the other white kids were. I'd never been given a colour before.

I woke. Starlight? Moonlight? I didn't think it would be a good idea to move around in the dark so I lay there. I tried to pray. What do you pray for? Sitting Bull had gone to Canada for a few years, Jimmy had said. But the Canadian government had abused him and his band so badly he returned to the U.S. He had become famous. Buffalo Bill signed him up for his Wild West Show and Sitting Bull wound up scribbling autographs. He even wore sunglasses for his old eyes. Jimmy had laughed: "But every Indian is a drunk, right?"

A story formed in the night before I fell back to sleep. I had scarcely any notion of writing one. I'd become bored with my journalism classes and was thinking about dropping out. Someone spoke in their sleep. The story would come to be published on the front page of the city paper. I would be invited to speak at various places about what had happened at the Knee. A friend who farmed would snort at my reporting: "Really unbiased. Yahoo for Sitting Bull and the Little Big Horn. Tears for Wounded Knee. If they want to be free, fine. Tell them to stop taking government handouts." A friend of my mother's would listen to my story as I told it to her in our living room. She would shake her head: "But they're the children of Ham. It may seem cruel but it's the judgement of a just God. The children of Ham will always be slaves to the whites. It's God's law."

The toe of a boot dug into my ribs.

"Let's go," Jimmy was saying, hanging onto his AK-47. "Maybe the truce is over and I'll need you for that shield."

A large white tepee had been erected and drums were beating. A crowd had gathered.

"It's a ceremony for those warriors who had their first fight Friday night. The warriors are blooded. You can watch. But don't go near the tepee. Powerful medicine flows from its entrance. A guard will knock your head off if you get in the way."

Shirts and jeans and Winchesters and semi-automatics and headbands and beads. They moved in single file, their feet shuffling with the drums. They came up to an old monument erected to those killed at the Knee a hundred years before. Each one placed their hand on it. Jimmy too.

"I joined AIM a few months ago," Jimmy was telling me later. "I knew they were planning this."

"So what's going to happen?"

"What can happen? Eventually, we'll have to surrender. There'll be no water, no food, no ammo. We'll last awhile though. It's spring."

"You don't think Nixon will negotiate. You think he'll answer with guns."

"Yeah. He will most probably. But we'll get a piece of him. Of all of you. Dark children of a White God."

"Jesus was a Jew."

"So?"

"He wasn't white."

"The traders with their whiskey were white. And the pony soldiers. And the preachers who called us devils."

"Indian tribes fought each other and lied and broke trust. That doesn't make native religion worthless in your eyes."

"There is nothing in the Christian's heart for the land, even though they claim God the Father made the land."

"Yes. God created. He told us to be caregivers for the earth and all that He made."

"Sure. And a lot of whites follow that, don't they?"

"You can't say every white is a Christian."

"I could blow you away. You think this is a seminary? We're fighting for our lives, not a bunch of doctrine. White Man's God."

The truce ended before we could drive out and that night the fire fell. Jimmy was smoking in the graveyard and telling me that the Quakers had been trustworthy in dealing with the Indians. Lights formed a sudden parabola over us. He pushed me flat behind a headstone. Then came the sound, not nearly as loud as in the movies: Tack-tack-tack-tack-tack.

Jimmy hunched over and ran and I stumbled after him. We dropped into a bunker. There was another man there, a friend of Jimmy's I'd met at the gas pump, Michael Many Wounds. Michael and Jimmy watched for the source of the U.S. fire and then opened up with their own tracers. The shots went where they wanted them to and they cheered. WHACK-WHACK-WHACK-WHACK-WHACK-WHACK. Now the noise hurt. I had a swift image from the afternoon of a Sioux woman, a flower of wrinkles, smiling and telling me Sitting Bull would be riding this night as she pressed hot bannock into my hand. Firing erupted from all over the valley and the hills. Then it ended. In the silence, one last shot.

"Thirty-thirty," grunted Michael.

"So, White Man's God," rumbled Jimmy, leaning back into the cool earth of the bunker. "What would you do?"

"Here?"

"If you were Sioux. Apache. Blackfoot. You're on your front lawn and they drive up and beat on your father and mother and on your grandmother, they throw you out of the house, rip up your garden, tie you up and tell you it's not your property anymore."

"I'd get a lawyer."

Jimmy laughed. "White Man's God and his lawyers and judges. No. There's no law for you. They just take. They rape your kid sister. Now what?"

"I fight back."

"Like us."

"I wouldn't stay on a reserve."

"You're going to leave the reserve? The Cheyenne tried that and the U.S. called out ten thousand soldiers to track them down. The Nez Perce tried it too. Of course, we're talking a hundred years."

"I'd go anywhere."

"The white man doesn't want you on his street."

"I'd get a good job."

"A white man's job."

"As soon as I'm doing it, it's my job."

"So easy. You grow up in a clean house with a green lawn and all your rosey options. But what if all your family and friends are on the reserve? What if it's your ancestral home? Try to think Indian, White Man's God. Try to feel it."

"People leave."

"Sure. I left."

"That was good, wasn't it?"

"For you everything is something to be used to get you farther and higher. I can't think like that. For Christians the whole earth is something to be used up."

"How can I think that way? All of God is in creation. It says His divine nature is in everything. You can see it. You can see Him. You get to know who He is just by looking. How can I desecrate what is part of him? It's Christ's face."

The bunker was so black I could not see them. Jimmy only grunted: "White Man's God."

All the next day there was firing from one end of the Knee to the other. Scarcely anyone moved from place to place. They were worried about snipers. A few crawled back and forth with food and water. Tim ended up in my bunker, his beard longer and scruffier. He was incensed.

"Did you know they put a bullet in the LTD?" he squawked. "What are we supposed to tell Hertz?"

"They can bill the President of the United States," grinned Michael Many Wounds.

At night we were free to walk. Jimmy took Michael and I back to the graveyard.

"If we get hit, it'll save us a trip," he smiled. He lit up. "I'll tell you something else you don't know, White Man's God. It was a white man went to Cochise. A Christian. I guess he was a real one. Usually the best white man is one that's shot and hung. But this man kept his word. He would read his Bible and pray every morning. Cochise saw that. And he treated the Apache with dignity and respect. He treated them as if they were also God-made, like all whites think white people are. He made the peace. He was a soldier too. I cannot understand that."

160

"What was his name?"

"Howard. Brigadier General Oliver Otis Howard."

"Why are you telling me all this?"

"I keep hoping there are others like Howard and like Penn and the Quakers. A few more whites who belong to God. Michael hears me talk all this crazy talk. No one else."

Michael grinned in the dark. "It's good crazy talk."

Jimmy's face was sparked by the cigarette. "I'd like a God who was God for everyone, not a Sioux God or a Piegan's Blackfoot God, not a white man's God or a Hindu's God or a Moslem's God. I think there has to be this Great Spirit for all peoples. Doesn't the Christian Bible say everyone is made of one blood, every tribe, every nation? So a priest told me when I was a boy. I want this God."

I squatted under a tree, its branches still sharp and bare. "I used to walk from my house in the suburbs to downtown, to Main Street. I wanted to see Indians."

"I'll bet you were always glad to get back to your home in the suburbs, weren't you?"

"I thought that if I were an Indian, I would return to the old ways. I would go back to the pride that used to be the Indian people before the alcohol came. I would break free and be a warrior once again. And the God I would worship would have the face of Jesus, dark with the sun of the desert. He would be the Great Spirit. I kept going back to Main Street. It depressed me. But it was something exotic at the same time. I wanted to tell them to go back to their dignity, to go back to their strength."

"You were one of the crazy whites who gets romantic about the Warrior of the Plains. But no people can go back."

"I had just become a Christian. I was only fourteen. But I thought a true Christian should be full of life. There should be rivers and mountains and immense prairies in them. Purple thunderstorms and long yellow seasons of the sun. Snow and ice and winds that soared. Stars so sharp they cut slits in the night. I read some of the Plains Indians' own writings. We had so much in common. Surely they could see Christ was a God for them, full of courage and sacrifice, strong with love and noble suffering, not afraid to die, not afraid to rise again, purifying everyone, restoring everything. I read that the Father God chose to make all the earth through Jesus. All the trees. All the beasts. All the winds and clouds and waters. This is your God, I told them, this is the One to rescue you. I said all this with my heart. That's why I keep telling you: The Indian should be what he was created to be. What the true Christ created him to be. What Father always intended him to be. But how often is this true God talked about?"

"When you talk crazy like this, what do your white friends say?"

"I had the Cree make me a buckskin shirt. I showed them the design I wanted. No buttons. I just pulled it over my head. It was a very light tan, all kinds of fringes, and just a sun and a moon on the front for decoration. It was a beautiful shirt. A man at my church saw it and he advised me to destroy the shirt because it was associated with native spirituality. No, I told him. I designed the shirt. The sun and the moon come from St. Francis of Assisi, who loved God's creation. Brother Sun and Sister Moon. This got me into more trouble. St. Francis was a Catholic and I was supposed to be a Protestant. Destroy the shirt, he said. It will bewitch you. The Indians are a downtrodden people because they worship false gods. I thought about this. I came back to him and I asked him what he thought white people worshipped. Jesus, he told me. No, I said, mostly they worship money and sex and power. Aren't these false gods?"

"What happened?"

"One day I left the church. There were other reasons as well."

"But you did not stop believing in your crazy Christ?"

"No. I could not."

"Or remaining among Christian people."

"There are Francises there. And Howards and Penns. You told me."

"Mmm."

"There are Indians who are Christians."

"Some. Apples. I'm not interested in sucking up to the whites. I want the real God who says I am equal with everyone. But is it Jesus? Is it Buddha?"

The sky erupted. Flares and tracers and the hammer, hammer, hammer of guns, fire scribbling across the night. The three of us ran to the bunker. As the AK-47s bounced against their shoulders, I covered my ears. Once a cluster of shells shattered the cement blocks near our heads and we hugged the bottom of the bunker.

"If you get shot," Jimmy told me as we lay in the dirt, "you can come back as an owl and tell me which God I should believe in. Okay?"

With the dawn came another truce.

"Get out," ordered Jimmy. "Tell our story. Here." He grabbed an orange bumper sticker that read, Wounded Knee, National Historic Site, and scribbled an address. "When I'm out of prison, write me. Go."

Tim was rounding everyone up. "It's only a three hour truce. We've got to move."

We piled into the car and started up the hill, toward the armored car and the young man with the machine gun. The FBI were there too. They would detain us for an hour, ask us question after question, until an old pro for U.S. News and World Report would persuade them to let us go. He put an arm around my shoulder and smiled: "It'll be worth it, son. You'll get your first by-line for this story." I could see Jimmy Strikes With A Gun and Michael Many Wounds still watching from below as we got back into the LTD. They must have seen me. No one waved.

I walked down Main Street in my home city and I felt stifled. I wished I could take all the Cree and the Metis from Main Street to the Knee. Let them be warriors again, I prayed. Let them want dignity and freedom more than anything else. No one at my church was interested in my story. The city paper published two articles and paid me and I got an A+ in reporting that term. I went on to seminary. My buckskin shirt was stolen, along with my luggage, the evening I flew into Vancouver to begin my studies.

The uprising collapsed many weeks after we left Wounded Knee. Only a few managed to escape the armed noose of the U.S. government. A few years later, in court, AIM successfully defended itself against the charges brought against it by the FBI over Wounded Knee. I saw a photograph of AIM leaders celebrating their courtroom victory with a huge cake strewn with candles. Sitting Bull and Crazy Horse and Spotted Elk I read about in books. I passed through my years as a white man's pastor. Some I met despised all Indians. Some loved all Indians. I met many Cree and Sioux and Blackfoot who had returned to their native spirituality and embraced it, drumming, drumming. I met others in churches. On special occasions, they dressed in white deerskins and eagle feathers. They drummed too, drummed that Jesus was the true God, the God for all peoples.

A hot wind. Cotton bursts over our knees. Jimmy buttons his shirt. He has shown me the massive scar tissue from an FBI bullet, like white plastic melted and waxy over his dark skin.

"I forgive them," he says. "They're just crazy white men." He grins. "White Man's God. All right. I will tell you. I follow the God of all peoples. But it is no white man's religion. No. The white man actually does pretty badly at it. This Christ, you know, he does not have a white bone in his body. What do you think?"

I laugh. "I think you are right."

We can only talk for an hour. He is in town for a Piegan pow-wow. White and blue and white the sky. It is strange to pray together. I see him with the AK-47: "I'm going to use this white guy as a shield and start blasting." There is a small Bible covered in deerskin in his shirt pocket, stained with dirt and sweat. He reads to me from it and the fingers on the white paper are strong. The sun over the Dakotas. The sun over the Rocky Mountains. A thousand years.

"It could have been Sitting Bull beside me. It could have been Spotted Elk," I say.

Jimmy saddens, his whole spirit seems to droop. "All the blood of my people. If someone had spoken well a hundred years ago. If someone had prayed well. No Washita. No Little Big Horn. No Wounded Knee. No white bodies. No brown bodies. Only one body, only God's body. Ah. I dream too much. Foolish dreams. Is this a world without suffering and death? Out of the broken soul, an eagle. Out of one tired to death, one who runs. Out of blood and nails, a life, all life. How else can Father work?"

Jimmy stands. "I have to go. There are things I need to say about Jesus at the pow-wow."

"I guess we won't see you again."

"No. I don't think so. Not here."

"God gave us the creek."

"Yes."

We embrace with strength. The wind has dropped and the air is quiet.

"Jimmy. What happened to Michael?"

He smiles gently in his sadness. The cottonwoods are a rich green.

They do not move. In the silence of the wind, you can hear the creek. Over stones, over sand, over time.

"Michael was killed a few days after you left. He is buried at the Knee. No. Don't speak. I must finish. He never forgot how you talked that last night. Prairies in you. Thunderclouds in you. A God of all peoples and beasts. The God for the Sioux and the Cheyenne and for the earth. The dying God. The God to free us. No white had ever spoken like this. He would joke about it just to keep it from his soul. The only good Indian, he would laugh, is a free Indian. When the bullets found him, he lived a few minutes. He wanted me to pray with him. How could I pray? I remembered the stations of the cross. I talked about the stations of the cross. I believed nothing. He believed everything. I buried him the next day. Alive. What else could he be? He clenched life in his dead hands and took it with him. I was the dead one. After the uprising ended, I had nothing. Except Michael. He haunted me. What he believed haunted me. When I had found my way to the truth, I came back. I put flowers at his grave and a new stone. There is a cross on it. And what he prayed at the end: "God of all bloods, I am Michael, your son." When you go back, White Man's God, you will find it. It is not obvious, but you will find it."

He begins to move off down the path. Now a warm breeze blows from the mountains and the cottonwoods rush overhead like a sea. Some bits of seed dance around us, bright as grains of starlight. The blue softens and moves over and around all the earth. Soon he is far away but he laughs as he crosses the wooden bridge over to the other side of the shining creek: "White Man's God. It is an evening for angels."

21

The Woodcutter

The woodshed could hold eleven cords of split and stacked wood and it was empty. Aaron scarcely noticed it as he strode, propelled by fury, into the retreat centre. It was not an impressive shed. He glimpsed a sagging roof and some crooked beams. The retreat centre, on the other hand, was solid and sure, boards and brick and stone and large windows that brought mountains and light and sky indoors. Aaron stormed through the front entrance.

The retreat director sat in a chair bigger than he was, eyes obscured by glasses spattered with sunlight. Aaron thought he looked like a ferret but opened up to him anyway. He ranted and raved about his church which had fired him, his elders that had abused him, his wife and children who had left him, his friends who had ignored him, his God who had abandoned him. The director said nothing. Once, in the middle of the tirade, he opened a drawer in his desk and, without taking his eyes off Aaron, plucked a Scotch mint from a bag and popped it into his mouth. After about sixty-five minutes, Aaron stopped, hands and face burning, hunting for a better word, a stronger phrase, an accusation more fierce.

"Have you ever chopped wood?" the director asked.

They gave Aaron a maul, an ax, a chainsaw. And eleven cords of wood in fifteen foot lengths. Simmering with adrenaline, he told the director he would saw the wood in one day and have the lot of it split within a week. He put in two hours before dark that first afternoon. It was early December. The sun set before five. The snow and grass were blistered with small, angry woodchips. They flew from him in swarms. But at five it was too dark to work, even for a man who was reckless. There was a great deal more to saw.

During supper he sat at a long wooden table with three staff members and another pastor named Skiff, who asked Aaron how long he would be at the retreat centre.

"One or two weeks," replied Aaron, jabbing at his grilled chicken. "Just enough time to get my head together and make plans to take another church. How about you?"

Skiff shrugged. "Another month maybe."

"Then what? Do you have another church lined up?"

"Oh, no. I've pastored twenty years and that's enough for me. I'll go into business. Insurance."

"But. What about your call?"

Skiff smiled and shook his head.

After an hour of communal prayer and Scripture reading the next morning, Aaron assaulted the woodpile with the chainsaw once more, chips snarling up from his fists. After lunch was free time.

"Read. Think. Hike. We can talk. You can work on the wood again tomorrow morning," the director suggested.

"No," cut in Aaron. "I have to finish the wood. I only have a couple of weeks."

Stars sprinkled the backs of his hands when he was done. They were calling him for supper, ringing a steel bar. He set down the chainsaw. He had trouble flexing his fingers and his hands shook. The smell of gasoline rose from his skin and his clothing. Tomorrow, he thought, it is just the logs and the ax. My bone and muscle and will against years and years, centuries of wood. Myself against the Maker of Trees.

The maul was heavy, almost three times the weight of the ax, and his first blows the next morning glanced off the logs erratically. But he was determined to use the maul on the larger logs so he kept at it until his swinging became more sure. As the solid hits grew in number and the logs split with cracks like gunfire, a peace settled over him.

It did not last. With the rhythmic work an iron door in his mind swung open and faces burst upon his imagination, conversations, rooms, pulpits, meetings, angry sentences, words of fire, memory after memory scraping him, cutting around and around so that he struck at the logs with a sudden explosion of rage, blasting through stout rounds with a single heft of the maul. The first day of chopping ended with a snowfall that seemed to scald his forehead and cheeks. He came to the table swollen with pain.

"How goes the battle?" asked Skiff.

"I must have been out of my mind to say I'd ever go back," spat Aaron. "Whipped like Jesus. Crucified like Jesus. By your friends. By Christians."

He sat at the window in his room, his light out. The snow had stopped and torn-up clouds hurried over and under a half-moon. The mountain range had taken on a pristine whiteness and the moon was strong enough to give it a sharp, full, three-dimensional effect, almost as if the peaks were pulsing and throbbing, rising and floating, reminding Aaron of the luminous blacklight posters of the Sixties.

"You create so much beauty out there," Aaron prayed. "Why can't you do it with the human heart?"

The more rhythmically he swung the maul, the more the memories boiled up from the stew of wound and bleeding and betrayal. He tried to concentrate on how his blows landed. He learned to look for the faint crack in the top of the log and strike that squarely. The best feeling he could produce in himself came when a log split cleanly and fell away neatly from the cutting stump. The satisfaction of that hummed through his blood and his bones and even his mind paused to swallow it in, as if it were a morsel of lush scenery.

But not every log split cleanly. Sometimes his blows were off-centre. Sometimes the maul blade sank into the round with a thud and apparently effected no change whatsoever. Sometimes he had to pull and pull and pry the maul loose. He learned to be wary of the logs lumpy with knots. He could strike and strike at some of these and get nowhere. Wedges would be used but frequently the wedges got stuck and it cost him more energy to drive the wedges out or through. He would pant and sweat even though it was fifteen below. The moments came when he wanted to quit. But he couldn't leave wedges in logs or blades embedded in thick, wet wood. He thought of the retreat director sucking his white Scotch mints. I'll be finished in a week, he'd told him. Yet he had to complete this before he left. Grunting, he yanked or beat the maul out of the knot-twisted logs.

"Some of you are hardly worth it!" he shouted.

It was important to finish each log, no matter what. It was a great victory to finally split the hardest ones in two. But there were clearly some which sapped all Aaron's strength and still remained truculent. Not many. A few. It was hard to take, but Aaron learned to recognize these logs after a few blows and would toss them aside and never approach them again. They took too much and rewarded him with very little. When stacking came, they would go into the shed whole. A long, slow burn for somebody one winter's night two years ahead. Someone holding the broken windows of faith in hands and shirt pockets, the fragments pricking and stabbing. Maybe a whole log would help. But to burn well, it would need a split piece too, dried by mountain wind. Maybe in the flame the hurting man, the dying woman would find God once more. Aaron had already burned other people's anger and pain in the wood they'd left behind. He hadn't seen much of God yet but at least his flesh had been warmed. Who were the others who had cut the wood two or three years before? Had that been a dry winter or an especially cold and snowful one? He imagined them battling the woodpile in blizzards, cheeks and ears whitening from frostbite. Now he burned their efforts. In the month of December, the burning of this split wood in his room was the only act that seemed holy to him, a sacrifice that mattered to God, the souls of others an incense drifting up to him. Who would burn his struggles, send flames over his spirit, toss the wood he cut out of his heart into the stove and then pull out a novel, or maybe even a Bible to read? Who would his wood heal?

The woodshed took on enormous proportions when he set up his first stack of split wood. The stack cringed there, dwarfish and inconsequential—it blew down Christmas Day when a chinook gushed through the mountain passes. There was a day of rain and snow and then a high pressure system slashed out of the Arctic, so that Aaron woke to a glistening marrow-red sunrise of forty below.

It took him an hour to restack the wood, which at least had been under cover and was dry. The rest, heaped about the woodshed, split or whole, was frozen together. He whacked at it with the back end of the maul head to loosen it up, his gloves ripping as he jerked the wood from its ice cradles. When the day ended his fingers were bleeding. This went on all through January. Freezing rain, followed by ice, followed by snow, followed by subzero cold. He broke the maul handle trying to force a log from a mass of wood all iced over. He had to use the smaller ax to split. The wood broke apart quickly because it was so cold. But what the maul had done in one blow took the ax three.

"I'll need a few more weeks yet," Aaron told the retreat director.

The director sat, hands folded in his thin lap, and nodded, sucking at a Scotch mint.

"I thought you'd be at your new church by now," smiled Skiff at the supper table.

"It's taking longer to do the wood," shrugged Aaron. "Snow. Ice. I need more time."

"What does it matter? Let someone else do it."

Other people came and went, on weekend retreats or day retreats. Pastors. Church members. No one Aaron knew. Some would laugh too much for him. Some would hover over fires and tables and shoulders like grey storms. Some were just taking a break. Some were hanging on for dear life. A few talked with Aaron. Sam was leaving the pastorate to go into accounting. John was returning to the military. Ben had had enough and was driving a taxi. Krystal was going into management with a big oil firm. Jerry sat with Aaron at the huge fireplace in the main lodge. The room was dark and the light flashed and flashed on their faces and bodies.

"What can I do?" The man stared into a sparking log. "I used to imagine Jesus huddled over fires like this with James and Matthew and Philip. What if they'd stopped? The heart killings came to them. But they rose from the dead. What if they'd put out the fire in the dark and gone home?"

Aaron clawed and chopped at the wood to free it from ice and snow. Then, his gloved hands slippery and shining, he would balance the logs on the stump and swing, silver spraying his face as the wood broke. Exhausted, he would end a day with an hour or two of stacking. When darkness poured over the mountains and over his eyes, the shed still looked large and empty. Eleven cords of wood. How much did he have cut and stacked now? Two or three, if he was lucky?

The days came when he didn't want to do it anymore. He'd had enough. The adrenaline had been scorched from his body weeks ago. Now he felt tired. Alone. But it was the sort of tired that does not let you rest. And he knew if he did not go to the woodpile he would not be able to seize the bone weariness that would give him sleep. He forced himself into the rich royal blue of sky and the clear cold that traced the pattern of his spine. Chop. Cut. He had thought he would dream of the wood but he never did. His dreams were full of colour and movement. No memories. No anger. No axes. No woodchips. Awake, he sat at the stove in his room and watched the stars fall gently. Wood from other tortured souls burned.

Weight melted from his body. His hair fell over his ears. Dirt worked under his skin and nails, water blisters broke and his palms thickened and yellowed. There was no one to care whether or not he grew a beard, so he let it come. Glancing into a mirror, he allowed himself a lopsided smile—he was perfect for a series of sermons on the Old Testament prophets.

February was a mercy. Yes, that was the only word that meant something. Dry and warm, chinook after chinook pulling golden fire over the foothills and forests. The wood loosened in the heat. He no longer had to break it out of its rock face of ice. Crack. Crack. The rounds split neatly, long grain exposed like a fine stone crystal. Scent rose through his being. He would chew the pale splinters for the flavour, sensing he was feeding on years as well as on minerals, on fresh resin in old trees nurtured by wind and frost and fast glittering meltwater.

He grew wearier. Sometime after Valentine's Day he was sure the shed was half-full. But it had taken him so long to get there he despaired of ever finishing the job. Well, other things had never been finished in his life. The wood could be left too. He could walk away and be a free man anytime he liked. He'd done enough. His wife had written him a letter. What was he thinking, she wanted to know. Should they continue the separation? Should they divorce? His denomination sent a curt typewritten letter—If he divorced he could no longer serve with them as a pastor. Would he like some counselling? His pension stood at forty thousand dollars.

"Everything in me is tired," he told Skiff. "But if I don't chop, I can't sleep."

"I've been praying for you."

"Thanks, Skiff."

"It's the terror that has to go, Aaron. I pray God will melt the ice that locks you in."

The ax flew, a shining head painted red. At five o'clock it was still light. At six the sun remained well above the horizon. March blustered over his head—snow flurries, some rain, some cold, but more light, more warmth, slowly, the earth turning, the sun drawing near, spring advancing like a green-speared army of deep intent.

Aaron pulled an old Bible down from the bookshelf above his woodstove. How long since he had read King James? It was like delving into Hamlet or Macbeth. He chiselled away at the Psalms and the gospel of Luke. He lay back on his bed, someone's wood work burning, the light snapping jaws on the ceiling, or no, was it David leaping in front of the ark?

"God," he would breathe in the dark, "Oh God, Oh Father."

Skiff met him at breakfast. "Some of us are doing a prayer walk each day to get ready for Easter. Would you like to join us?"

Aaron shook his head. "It's good of you. But Easter is where the trees and the fallen wood are. I have to be there."

Another stack went up, skimming the ceiling. Perhaps it was possible. The ax plunged into smaller logs now. Shorn, pieces dropped left and right from the stump. Carefully, he would build up the wood walls within the shed, as if erecting a stone wall without mortar. He had learned how to shore up the ends by laying the wood in alternate patterns. Wood stacked in December and January took on the colour of honey. Greener wood was dark and stained. Round and split, small and large, knotted and smooth, clean split or ragged, the wood rose up from the ground, filling the shed.

He was no longer tired. Perhaps it could be done. If he stuck it out. He stood back frequently to look at the woodshed and its swelling substance. There is a beauty to this, how the wood fits together, he thought. Yet surely it was random. But how the symmetry then, the wholeness, the completeness? Out of January and the killing winter dark, how this?

April. He took Easter communion at the shed, sitting amidst the tall wood as if in a cathedral. He chewed the bread carefully. Drained the ceramic cup. Took a splinter of fresh birch and placed it between his teeth. Jesus and wood. Carpentry and killing. Tables, chairs, and crosses. Wood fire and light in all darkness.

Forgive me, he wrote his wife and children.

Forgive us, she responded.

Yes, yes, he penned in the light of another's cross.

Let us love one another, he wrote the church. Even if I never preach to you again. Let us love one another.

Yes, responded the church.

May I have another chance? he wrote the denomination. May I be as one who serves? May I try to live the evangel somewhere? May I learn to shepherd and lay down my life for the sheep? May I try again to be like Jesus and not hide the wounds?

But the denomination did not respond.

"The wood is praise," Aaron told Skiff.

They sat on a bench drenched in mountains and crystal clear sunlight. Skiff smiled, gnawing on an O Henry bar.

"Perhaps it's time to go out then," Skiff said.

Aaron shook his head. "I must complete it."

"Let another take on that joy."

"It won't mean anything to them, just to cap off my work. Let them have their own vocation. Then it will mean something."

"A cathedral was not built in one lifetime. Not by one man."

"Some of this is second growth forest. Others planted it. Others cut it and drove the logs here. But it's my task to split and build. All of it. This is what I give to God. It is all of my days. Years from now, at night, in terror, cold and alone, a man or a woman will carry the wood to their room and they will pray by its light, cry by its flame, hear God in the cracking of the poplar and birch, hope again after a week, a month, a hundred nights. It is what I have to give them. I can never know them. But we are going to Jerusalem together."

Skiff nodded. "I ought not keep you from your worship any longer then."

"Are you still going into insurance?"

"Sure. Insurance against evil. I'm staying with the Lord, Aaron. His walking. His campfires. His parables. His cross. And the resurrection of the dead—I've always wanted to find out how that fish tasted he grilled on the beach. When the morning finally comes, I'll be with him for breakfast."

And you could say the ax sang to God in the flash of its swing. That Aaron praised God as the wood rose to heaven. That he would not stop until it had been done and every log, every stick had found its niche in the house of God he fashioned within the eleven cord shed. That it sounded so crazy to him to think and act this way over a pile of wood. And it was so crazy. It must have been Jesus smearing dark mud and God's spit over his eyes, fully blinding him and telling him to wash off the blindness in the pool of Siloam.

Mare's tails shot out crimson, snapping with the coming of the light. Aaron stood looking at the cords of wood, reluctant to leave, having replaced a final piece of maple which had fallen with several dozen others during the night. The ax was propped against the stump. For another, he thought. Then he turned to go into the main lodge and the retreat director was behind him.

"That's all," said Aaron. "I can leave this morning. I'm meeting my wife for coffee in town."

The director nodded. Blood light glistened over his glasses as the sun slipped up the mountain slopes. A warm wind puffed out his plaid shirt from his scarecrow frame.

Aaron looked back at the shed. "It has to be like the wood, doesn't it? Bit by bit, cutting, stacking, ice, snow, another stack, another stack, some days ready to fly like a swallow, others just wanting to fall to your death. The splinters dig into your skin, the cold, the doubt rips at your mind. You try to pray, you try to worship, and you add another piece, and nothing is happening, you look and you look for God, and surely nothing can be happening. Jesus presses on to Golgotha. Paul presses on to Rome. Somehow we learn that God is most true when the dark is most real. All I did was swing an ax. I became a free man. Just one day after stacking another piece of a thousand pieces. I became the cathedral. It's your whole life and maybe you'll recognize it. Maybe another generation will see the cathedral."

Now it was morning. The director had his hands in his pockets. But one arm reached up and around Aaron's shoulders and a surprising strength pressed Aaron into the director's skin and bone and life and the scent of garlic and earth, for the director worked in the greenhouse during the winter and in the garden during the summer. And there was the scent of Scotch mint. The director propelled Aaron toward the lodge as a cloud moved and the morning star, not yet obscured by the common day, lit up like a match head over the white mountains.

"Come and have breakfast," the director said.

22

Commodities

She woke in the dark, the clock's face casting a green stripe of light over her small face. She showered and dressed, kissed her sleeping husband and son, and took the smaller car, backing out into the wet street.

The new store was on the other side of the city. She beat most of the rush hour traffic and had crossed to the west end by seven o'clock. Grabbing a coffee and a muffin from 7-11 she drove to the new store and parked. She was an hour early. Now that the driving had stopped she yawned and fought off a desire to sleep. The coffee helped, hot and black and thumping its way through her blood. The sun cut itself free of the stars and the night and slit the air for a sudden flaring and spilling of light. She prayed happily as the sky blued, a peace and a freshness seeping all through her as the colours of the earth slipped off the winding scarves of the dark.

The others drove up, dozens and dozens of cars and trucks. She checked her makeup in the visor mirror and got out to say hello. They laughed with one another as the day's warmth stroked them. A great red ribbon was being fastened across the smoked glass doors of the store. The building was as big as a warehouse. The Costco of Christianity, the brochure had said.

It was eight-fifteen. A spokesman with an economy-sized smile and a face and a skin that was the colour of teflon, she thought, stood above them on the concrete steps, just next to the wheelchair ramp.

They appreciated the pastors and Christian Education leaders and Sunday School teachers coming out for this special dedication of the new store, he said. In token of this appreciation there would be a special gift for each of them at the conclusion of the tour, along with a colourful packet to take back to their churches. The grand opening would be next week, Extreme Spirit Week. Church staff would receive a 10% discount off every item purchased, seven days a week, 12 hours a day.

Seven pastors prayed. It was eight-forty-eight. The ribbon was cut and an enormous woman she didn't know read a verse from Nehemiah about the completion of the wall around Jerusalem. The doors swung open.

The finest plastic, the teflon spokesman was saying. The highest quality imitation wood. Reproductions second to none. They shuffled after him down the massive aisles, craning their necks at shelving that soared to distant ceilings. Books over here, he told them. CDs there. And CD-ROMs with the computer section. Crosses and fridge magnets and drinking mugs and all the rest of the Christian art down this aisle. Toys on the mezzanine. Robes and chalices and communion cups were located there as well. Videos were situated by the Daily Bread Bakery. Bibles by the HE BREWS coffee shop. Three-D available by the theatre—shows every hour on the hour. JESUS in IMAX. Exceptional skin tone. Noah's Fish 'N' Chips in the FIVE LOAVES AND TWO FISHES section, along with The Wedding Feast Of The Lamb dining room, The Twelve Apostles Ice Cream Emporium, and Ezra's And Esther's Chili Dogs And Cheeseburgers. Men's clothing. Women's clothing. KIDZ KLOTHED IN CHRIST. Elijah Trek Biblical Camping Gear. Hardware. Automotive. Eden Lawn And Garden Equipment. Scriptural Sporting Equipment: Hermon And Horeb Snowboards, Gennesaret Rods And Reels, Peter and Andrew Lures, Moses Drivers and King Saul Putters, Extreme Spirit bats and balls and gloves. Our Messiah Marina at the waterfront will be featuring King David sailing craft, Pneuma and Ruach powerboats with Spirit engines, and a whole line of dinghies and canoes.

Down this aisle we have the Adam and Eve line of women's cosmetics and men's toiletries. A health spa with state of the art equipment and plenty of free weights and a sauna (an additional membership is required). Whirlpool tubs from Jordan Blessings Products. Also their entire line of baptismals, from the Rocky Mountain Whitewater and the Prairie Sweetgrass models, all the way to the highly popular simulations of the Jordan River, the Sea of Galilee, the Nile, and the Red Sea—installed in your church free of charge. Nehemiah Construction has several show homes at the end of this annex. This particular home features an actual planetarium ceiling—you can choose the Christmas Eve Sky or the Resurrection Sky or the spectacular Parousia model. A games room is in this annex. We have the purest board games and top of the line pool and ping-pong tables.

There are seven more annexes, three of which are completed. One is the Bethlehem annex, our Christmas specialty store. Another annex has the Good Friday Shop for Easter supplies. The other annex houses Biblical Brides. We have plans this year for a pet shop, a bowling alley, a paint ball complex, and a Jericho Climbing Wall. In the future, we hope to have an indoor midway featuring Biblical rides like Noah's Flood, the Tower Of Babel, the Plagues, the Red Sea, Donkey Ride To Bethlehem, Walking On Water, The Last Judgment, and Gehenna. The future is unlimited really. Unless Jesus returns, ha ha. There will be an insurance agency and a travel agency, an investment firm, a medical and dental clinic, two law firms, and a chapel. We'll provide round the clock pastoral care for sales staff, customers, and night shift management and stockroom personnel. The chapel will provide worship services for all Sunday shoppers. So you see, the best is yet to come.

She sensed vertigo coming on and was grateful they were invited to take a seat at the HE BREWS coffee shop for a complimentary beverage and a slice of angel food cake. The pastors she sat with were saying how incredible it all was. She could scarcely think. A glossy packet was placed at her elbow by a handsome young man in a crew cut dressed in red, white, and blue. A steaming coffee soon followed, black, carried on a tray by a pretty young woman in a white Biblical robe. Hoping it might restore perspective, she drank her coffee quickly. But Mr. Teflon was speaking again.

He pointed out that there had been a central and enclosed staircase they had omitted from the tour. Heads nodded. It was time to take that staircase now and conclude the tour in style. By next week the glass elevator would be running. He apologized that today they would have to use Jacob's Ladder. She was fit but many of the others grunted and groaned their way to the top. They found themselves in a blue carpeted room with no chairs or sales goods, just one stylishly modelled PC. Mr. Teflon's smile expanded.

This is the future of our faith, he said. A man they had not noticed seated behind the PC ran his fingers over the keyboard like a pianist. Instantly men were standing in front of them, dressed in robes and rough tunics and sandals, all of them bearded and swarthy. One of them came forward and in a husky voice introduced himself as Peter. He asked them if they would like to go fishing in his boat. Another introduced himself as James and he said that his boat was also available, there would be plenty of room. Everyone could cross to the other side of the lake. Suddenly waves were rolling blue and white up to their feet and several pastors jumped back, afraid their shoes would get wet. The bearded men were pushing four boats toward them, water sloshing against the men's thighs. Peter looked back over his shoulder and told the others to wait. The Master is coming, he said. Across the water, light playing all over him, came a man walking. As he drew closer the men greeted him, calling him a rabbi. He walked right up to the tour group and smiled. Shalom, he said. Then he began to greet each person by their actual names. He looked directly at her and his eyes shimmered blue.

"Chelsea," he said in a warm voice.

She could not stop herself from responding: "Master."

"I am the Way, the Truth, and the Life, Chelsea."

Then he smiled and turned to the man standing next to her, an Orthodox priest. She put a hand over her eyes. God, she breathed. God. God. God. God. God.

The bearded men were gone. Mr. Teflon's smile grew larger. Can you imagine how software like this is going to revolutionize your Sunday School, your Christian Ed. program, your Sunday services? Your children will never be bored again. They can talk directly to David or Jonathan or Daniel or Isaiah. They can fish with Peter and Andrew. They can be there at the Transfiguration. At the Crucifixion. At the Resurrection. If your pastor has an off Sunday, Jesus himself can preach the sermon. You can be at the first Christmas, at Pentecost and be filled with the Spirit, at Armageddon. You won't need books or your imagination anymore. The name of this software program is SEEING IS BELIEVING and this is truly a whole new way of faith, a much better way. The shift we are talking about here is tantamount to a new Reformation. Millions are going to be saved. This is not simply virtual reality, like one of your computer games on your home PC. This is enhanced or augmented reality. In fact, this is Christian reality, as real as Jesus and our faith is going to get for us this side of an actual Heaven.

Now the entire holographic software program of the Bible is close to twenty-eight thousand U.S. But you can purchase it by the book at a thousand dollars a pop. If you want to take advantage of the savings that are yours when you buy the complete set, we certainly have financing available for your church. And the kind of PC you'll need to run the program, along with the holographic equipment, is all in stock at our computer store at very reasonable prices.

Your friends at church aren't going to believe what you just saw here. So we're giving each of you a free software package of the Gadarene demoniac. The incident where all the pork goes over the cliff, ha ha. Celinda and Priscilla will hand you the software as you leave the building. Let's close this special tour in prayer—and please remember to tell your people that there's no need to shop anywhere else. ALPHA AND OMEGA is the beginning and end for all your Christian end time shopping needs.

Chelsea called in to the church office and explained that she wouldn't be in. Then she drove to a nearby park and sat in the sun, holding the software package between her strong brown fingers. She went home and made supper. When her son came home she clung to him and started to cry. In bed that night her husband asked her what was wrong. How had her day gone? She spoke briefly about the holograms. He laughed. It was just moving pictures. People knew the difference between what was real and what was an image. She was overreacting. He rolled over and fell asleep. She thumbed through her Bible but could not read it. Her fingers clicked off the lamp. In the dark, his eyes came to her again. Not the Master's eyes. Not the blue eyes. The other ones. The eyes of a man behind him, the eyes of a man with a leather money bag. His eyes had been the last eyes she had seen. They had cut into her own eyes. But his eyes had not been him. No. Someone else was glittering out of them. It was like webs in the blackness, shining moonlit webs in the blackness.

She woke in the dark, the clock's face casting a green stripe of light over her small face. She showered and dressed, kissed her sleeping husband and son and took the smaller car, backing out into the wet street.

The new store was on the other side of the city. She beat most of the rush hour traffic and had crossed to the west end by seven o'clock. Grabbing a coffee and a muffin from 7-11 she drove to the new store and parked. She was an hour early. Now that the driving had stopped she yawned and fought off a desire to sleep. The coffee helped, hot and black and thumping its way through her blood. The sun cut itself free of the stars and the night and slit the air for a sudden flaring and spilling of light. She prayed happily as the sky blued, a peace and a freshness seeping all through her as the colours of the earth slipped off the winding scarves of the dark.

23

The Emperor of Ice Cream

Reverend Joel Coulter was feeling pretty good as he drove his white Lexus to the church that Sunday morning in Denver. The board had agreed to his salary increase, the new sanctuary was up, the new computer was in his office, and ten more families had joined the church in the past week: "This church impresses us so much, pastor. You people are really going somewhere." Yes, thank you, Lord, the bad old days were far behind him. As he turned off the expressway he permitted himself a moment of bad memories: Two churches where the pay had been poor, the people few, his prospects grim. There had been an office with no windows at the first church. One day he hadn't even been aware that a blizzard had struck the town until he had gone out the front door to head for home. He was snowed in so he spent the night sleeping behind the pulpit and two large potted plants.

He shuddered. Never enough to pay the bills. Few meals at restaurants. No tickets to the ball games. Hardly any new books. He closed the memories down. Enough. That was history. Now he had an office big enough to park a minivan in, seasons tickets for all the Broncos' home games, plenty of food on the table for his kids, and a congregation large enough to fill a small town. Thank you, Jesus. He turned into the immense parking lot and parked in the space lettered PASTOR JOEL. He stepped out of the car and surveyed his domain.

Three city blocks. Sanctuary. Day care. Gym. Pool. Movie theatre. Chrome and glass sparkled, warm red and yellow bricks glowed. He could see the Rockies from his office. When the congregation had topped 8000 the board had thrown in a season's ski pass. Lord, life was good. Best of all, he didn't even have to preach that morning.

He met the guest speaker in his office. The man was seated among the brightly tied and suited elders and he seemed small and large at the same time. His body was slender but his eyes were enormous and dark and they glittered as if an immense Rocky Mountain midnight, sizzling with stars, rose out of his soul. His handshake was strong and dry, his skin dusky.

"Bob Cameron," the man said.

"Reverend Joel Coulter," Joel replied. "Welcome. You were in missions where?"

"The Sahara Desert. With the Bedouin."

"Right. You saw God do some incredible stuff, I'll bet."

"Yes, Joel. Yes, I did."

"How big was the church there when you left?"

"It was about fifty. God blessed us."

"Were you there for a few months or a summer mission or what?"

Bob Cameron smiled, the teeth small and white in his twilight skin. "I was there for thirty years, Joel."

One of seven soft rock bands led the worship, ending the singing with the explosion of a purple and white smoke bomb and a song about the shekinah glory of the Lord. Joel emerged from the mists with several announcements, prayed for the offering, dismissed those ten years old and younger for junior church, and introduced Bob Cameron the missionary as Robert of Arabia, laughing with all his teeth, the polished teeth that matched his suit, his Lexus, and the whites of his eyes.

Bob Cameron came forward in a black short-sleeved shirt, white Levis, and sandals. He spoke gently. He spoke warmly. Half-way through he invited his wife up to share and together they began to sing a chorus in Arabic. It was shrill and high-pitched and when his wife suddenly trilled sharply with her tongue, Bob exploded, jumping up and down and crying, "Hi! Hi! Hi! Hi!" After the song, Bob spoke again, in conclusion, but Joel had a hard time focusing on the closing words. He was concerned that the missionary might start leaping up and down again and trilling in Arabic. Already one elder in the front pew had arched an eyebrow. When it was apparent that Bob was soft-spoken

Bob again, Joel relaxed. And that was when the words struck.

"In twenty-five years we never saw one Bedouin tribesman come to Jesus Christ. In twenty-five years not even one came to our tent to ask us more about Jesus. They listened to our messages by their camels and at the oases and they went on with their lives. In twenty-five years we counselled no one, baptized no one. For twenty-five years we sang our songs to God alone. But to God we sang them, not to thin air, for we saw him face-to-face, and his glory was each day burning like a pillar of fire in the Arabian sky. We ate and drank with God. We slept under God's grace. We woke drenched in his light and in anticipation of more of his love. We were Abraham. We were Moses. We were Paul. We were in a splendid desert and there was no clutter, no traffic, no cell phones, no schedules. There was so much room for God. And in the twenty-eighth year we baptized our first tribesman, Ali. What a glory. What a life. Oh God, I thank you, oh our living God, our blazing God, our Almighty mighty God who sees and saves!"

Joel was supposed to close the service with a prayer or an altar call or something. He stumbled to the microphone and mumbled. A husband and wife staggered to the front and knelt, weeping. Bob Cameron went to them and prayed. Joel walked through a door and down the hall to his office. Who was supposed to take care of the missionaries? Him? His wife and children were visiting the grandparents in Tampa. No, it was the Mickelsons, Art and Judy. Thank God.

After a few minutes he had collected himself enough to greet people and wish them God's blessing. He said goodbye to the Camerons. The dusky missionary winked as he took Joel's hand: "If you ever need a camel or an oasis or a desert, give me a call."

Joel spent the day alone, tinkling ice cubes in a tall glass of iced tea, on the back deck with its great view of the Denver skyline. He saw nothing. He was in his mind. He was trying to remember when he had sounded like Bob Cameron. He was trying to remember when he had believed like Bob Cameron. While he'd been at seminary, definitely. During his first church in New Mexico, in that dusty little town, what was it called, yes, all the stars of God's heaven had seemed to chime in his soul then. He had prayed prayers like gleaming, molten lava, formed new mountains, seen old ones shaken and removed, all in a happy, bright morning glory of God.

It occurred to him that the church in Denver had been built without much prayer. *Which just goes to show you,* he thought. *Goes to show you what?* retorted his mind. That churches can get big without prayer just like MacDonald's and Dow Chemical and the Mafia?

Joel spent the evening flicking through the channels on his fifty inch surround-sound TV and finally gave up. "Suppose I prayed like Bob Cameron," he said out loud. "Then what?" A book lay by the TV guide on the black coffee table: The Emperor of Ice Cream. Krystal, his wife, was taking a course on American poets. The one and only emperor is the emperor of ice cream. Wallace Stevens. And then he had a ludicrous image of himself and the entire church complex totally sculpted out of ice cream by some master chef. There he was stiff and white, face frozen in a smile. Well, not exactly white. He was sculpted out of cookie dough ice cream, his daughter Shara's favourite. So were all the buildings. Bright and perfect and absolutely lifeless. Then the sun poured its heat and light over the sculptures and everything began to melt, himself included, his eyes dropping into his neck, his entire body melting into a slick pool on the floor. The emperor of ice cream.

At one in the morning he was rolled up in Krystal's crimson throw on the black leather couch in the den. He could see a few stars through the sliding glass doors. All right, God, he said. Let's talk again. Let's spend some time together. Morning, noon, and night. Show me your glory.

Within a month, the size of the congregation began to decrease. The more Joel prayed, the smaller the church got, the fewer the number of people who showed up on Sunday mornings. In six months, the congregation was down to 4000. In a year of more honest prayer than Joel had ever prayed in his entire life, the weekly figure stood at 1500. After eighteen months, it was 675. He kept praying. "God," he cried out, "what are you doing to me? Is this what you call your glory?" A week later he was fired as pastor. "Sorry, Joel," an elder said, clamping an arm around his shoulders. "I don't think you're God's man for the hour anymore. But I hear the Broncos might be looking for a team chaplain. Why don't you look into that? And Wal-Mart is hiring too."

Joel was hit with a storm of pain and depression, but also, in more subdued moments, a curious sense of release. Krystal spent long evenings listening to him and helping him talk.

"What do you think happened, El?" she asked one night over hot apple cider.

"They said my sermons had changed."

"In what way?"

"They used to be upbeat and relevant. But they got too spiritual. An elder said the people were getting overdosed on God."

Krystal laughed. "Overdosed on God? Sounds like a good way to go, El."

And Joel, despite the crushing sense of failure that haunted him day and night, looked at her head-tilted-back laughter and gleaming copper hair, and smiled.

He spent the fall hiking in the mountains, something he hadn't found time for since moving to Denver. The aspens filled him with a clear light. Once, under a motionless blue sky, a pang of sun and coolness and warmth in each breathing moment, he lifted his hands in a shower of sparks, a shower of bright yellow aspen leaves, and in the silence of their falling he thought he heard: "This is my glory."

Another time he hiked with his family to a mountain lake. He and the three children wrestled and tumbled in the tall brown grass and he tickled them and the laughter struck the freshly whited peaks and Krystal jumped in and pinned him and all the play, all the touching and laughter felt so strange to him, but so good and strong, he thought: I am living another man's life. And in his son Jordan's laughter that came back to him from the snow and the granite and the flashing glacial water, he thought he heard: "This is my glory."

Once he was chatting with a neighbour as he was raking leaves and the man asked him about the job loss and the changes in Joel's life. They sat and drank bottles of Evian that Joel had placed on the front steps. The wind stirred the yellow mounds and tossed the leaves back over the grass. Joel was honest and his neighbour was startled: "It's been difficult for you, Joel. But you are a happy man." Joel shrugged. His neighbour nodded, staring at Joel. Suddenly he went to his knees in the bright blowing leaves and groaned, "Come to me, God, come to me, I'm sorry, come to me," and he cried. Joel, stunned, found his eyes hot and stinging, and he prayed with the man, and there had been no formula, no agenda, no pre-arranged plan, it had simply been his story, and this had never happened before, and the man was alive, alive. In the man's strong arms, hugging Joel, clutching desperately to life in the wind and the leaves, Joel ignored the neighbours who stood and watched from their yards, felt the man's birth, and thought he heard: "This is my glory."

The snows came and he was hired on as a ski instructor. Late one afternoon he had finished his classes and gone for a long run through powder. The sun was setting and the slope was a deep blue. He sank and fell and lay on his back. A cloud drifted over to obscure the first few stars. It seemed as if pins of light pricked his skin as he stared upward at the vast sky—ice crystals, coming slowly out of miles of winter air and touching him. His face became a white veil and he closed his eyes. Thank you, God, thank you, Jesus. And in the prayer of his gratitude, in the crystal of the young night, he thought he heard: "This is my glory."

In time, a group began to meet in Joel and Krystal's home. He had planned nothing. He had only prayed, and become, and for the first time in his life neighbours were sitting in his living room and praying to Jesus and reading the Bible and enjoying the presence of the living God. For six months there was only eight of them. In a year, nineteen. After two years, fifty-seven. The more he prayed, the more slowly the church grew. But the day came when they had to rent a hall, there were seventy of them, and into a life that had been free, dread made its heavy tread felt. Joel cried out to God, "I don't want a large church. I don't want our church to grow." The more he prayed, the more slowly the church grew. But one morning he woke up and there were over two hundred people. The day they voted to build he had them stand and hold hands, Krystal on his left, Bryanna, his oldest, on his right, and they prayed they would never be a building but a people. It occurred to Joel as he stood with his arms outstretched that he, and all of them, had assumed the posture of crucifixion. In that hall, in that praying, in those tightly held hands, in that posture, Joel thought he heard: "This is my glory."

The cross did come, and the nails, and Joel continued to pray, and the fresh pain did not destroy him, and the church's growth did not destroy him, and the building they erected did not destroy him. When they eventually plateaued at 408, Joel prayed, and the congregation shrank to 190 over the next year. Joel smiled and hiked into the mountains, purity searing his lungs, his face sweating and shining. God was in the mountains. But he was also in the city below. God was in his daughters and in his son and in his wife. He ate and drank with God. His life did not depend on numbers, it was not limited by his enemies, it was not defined by an increase or decrease of pain, these had no power over him. God was in his breathing, in the slow beating of his heart. God was the brightest flower of his dreams. And when a year came rushing upon him that carried with it Krystal's death, and he fell into a dark grief, there was a glory he had never seen, glistening in the blackness, and he emerged believing in a living, breathing Heaven. When his children moved away he was seized by another blackness and there came once again the choice to believe or to cease to believe. But one night a granddaughter named Krystal was placed in his arms and he blessed her, and in her eyes, and in the blessing, was God, and in all this there was a home once more and Joel lived on.

The church plummeted to less than a hundred people and it reminded Joel of the good old days and he laughed. And God's glory was in that laughter. Later the church swelled to five hundred or more and Joel shrugged and smiled and said, "Whatever, my God," and the glory of God was in the shrug and in the smile, the glory of God was in Joel's freedom. In all those years of mountains and skies and hopes and dreams and crosses, not once did the church become the building, and Joel slept and woke under the love of God, even during the bitter struggles and the long silences. It came to Joel, in his eighties, that somewhere on his way to Heaven his life had become rich and lovely, a joy. Roses weighed down the thorn bushes. And when his heart let him go, it was under a cataract of stars, midway through a tall mountain night, and as Joel had known, it simply meant there was less distance to cover to see the glory. The church, the people of God, remained divided, one part in heaven, one part on earth, and so it remained divided between heaven and earth, alive in its joys and in its crucifixions, until the end of time came to Denver.

24

The Legends of the
Green Chapels

What went wrong? Did we dream too much? Did we think we could never make mistakes? I think it is because everyone wanted to be right but no one wanted to be kind. We wanted to do great things, but to have mercy was not considered a great thing. We did not wish for integrity or maturity or the soft-skinned fruit of the Spirit. We wanted earthquake and wind storm and fire. No one wanted a whisper. We would not be humble. We would not be gentle. We would not be meek. And so we did not inherit the earth. We lost it.

I will write you only this one letter, Khartoum, my good brother. I scarcely have the time for it. You ask me why I am in this God-forsaken land? But I am in the desert of Moses and Elijah and Jesus. No land on earth could be less forsaken by our Lord. I am under the broom tree. It is the most excellent place to be. In this present Dark Age I have a few books and parchments, as the old ones say, and I hope I have enough that Christianity may flower again in another generation. How did we fail, my brother, how did we fail? Why is it that we wanted heaven on earth? We gave ourselves the best clothes and the best houses and the best salaries. Why is that no one wanted to be like Christ who for our sakes became poor? Why did our passion die? How did the body become more important than the soul? Why would none of us go into the ghetto or the jungle for the love of God?

You ask me if I am fed by ravens. No. By angels. What else when you are under the broom tree? Some water. Some bread. Some sleep. They come as translucent as a breeze. Scarves of white floating in a zephyr. One had eyes as green as emerald. Have you ever looked into a tiger's eyes? Yes, they can frighten. They are larger than life and death. As if the sun crashed into the earth and spoke. But the gentleness is there with the strength. Why could we not learn that? Why was it that the people of God committed themselves to the leaders who screamed at them the most? So that the meek perished? The men and women who could have saved us died in obscurity while the charlatans grew fat and bellowed the louder. A bruised reed Christ himself would not break. But we. But we—what reeds are left?

I can hardly concentrate enough to write. It is prayer I came here for. The sort of prayer our generation laughed at. All right, pray, we mocked. But then do something. As if speaking with God were nothing. We ran our souls into the ground for buildings and parking lots. Our churches were the bricks and glass. Not the people. And now the Church itself is dead because we fashioned her with money and mortar. How impressive North America's churches were, like the fine architecture of Rome, like the fine frescoes of the Sistine. But not finer than the souls God has fashioned. So our Lord allowed the rulers of this world to take our buildings and our land and to tax our silver until we were broken.

You ask me why God has abandoned us? Because he was not our God. Luxury and comfort and arrogance and vanity presided at our altars. We chose the luxurious careers, the sumptuous homes, the fattest investments. While the God fashioned were damned. What did it matter to us? We didn't believe in life after death anymore. Not heaven and hell. Not darkness and light. A fine restaurant was paradise enough. A good book. Television. Computer games. Our temples to our pleasures rose over the bones of our generation. Why did we not fear God?

Come to me here, my good Khartoum. Then I could cease from writing. I wish to pray for God's mercy like Daniel did. We thought the Church could never be shattered. Never exiled. Never diminished. Now it is an American diaspora. We are dispersed over the earth. Refugees. Homeless. Will our Chinese brothers take us in? How about the East Indian Christians whom we said were poor because they had no faith? Will the Jews help us? Or those among the Moslem nations who watched their fathers and mothers die for Jesus long ago while we gloried in our renewal movements and our in worship and in our healings?

Where will you be in a few months? How will this letter ever reach you? Eventually the government will force you out. You will wander and wander. What country on earth would take in a Christian refugee in this day and age? We will all die. Like the children of Israel who disobeyed in the journey between their salvation and their paradise. Our jaw bones will bleach in the wilderness. We will cry out to God but he will not answer.

But I pray. A remnant. Perhaps he will be gracious and leave us a remnant. Or stronger, younger, more faithful hands, purer hands than mine, will pry these books from my fossil and souls will sing for joy at what God has written. Or maybe they will weep. Maybe it will be as it was in Ezra's day. Who will rebuild the Church, my good Khartoum? It will not be our generation. Between Egypt and the Promised Land we transgressed. Another generation will see Canaan. We had our eshkol of the belly, our milk and honey of the senses. Our children and their children will taste of God's Spirit. And we thought we had so much of God's Spirit, didn't we, Khartoum? But, for the most part, it was only ourselves. We could not distinguish between God's Spirit and our own. Indulgence had blunted our faith. Oh, Satan will die for this deception. But we will die first.

The dark angels torment me. It was not enough what happened in America. They followed me here. Sometimes it is just a thought. Sometimes a dust devil or a stinging sandstorm. Some of them come to me with their eyes scorched, as if a hot poker had blazed into their sockets. Others are very beautiful, like dawn or a moonrise. I beat them off like a flock of vultures. What can they tempt me with? I satiated myself in Laodicea. I only wish to pray. Michael and Gabriel supply me with food and drink. I don't desire anything else. Perhaps a thicker blanket for the desert nights. Yes, the demons have tempted me with that, they with their strong limbs and agate eyes and dusky smiles. A warm fire. A woollen blanket. Thick socks. A cup of hot black coffee. I confess I could throw away my soul for warmth and comfort once the sun sets. But we threw away our souls for just that, long, long ago, didn't we, my good brother Khartoum? Now we pray and try to make amends. I cry out, I say, like Daniel: Are the seventy years accomplished? Can we restore the Temple and rebuild the walls? Is there a Cyrus for us?

The desert is not empty as you suppose, my good Khartoum. It is always full, always pouring out and always being replenished. Once or twice I am sure I have glimpsed God. He is not dead, as some Laodiceans suppose. It is the Laodiceans who are dead. That is why disaster fell upon us like a cougar springing from a thicket. We gazed into heaven, waiting for him, and when we could not spot him, we decided to engineer his return, just as we had sought to engineer his Spirit in our worship. Who was this year's Antichrist? What did the year 2000 signify? What would happen in Jerusalem? Who was Gog? When was Armageddon? Would it be more prudent and holy to invest in gold or in real estate or in spring water during the end times? Now we are in rags and stumble from nation to nation carrying our coffins upon our backs and still he has not returned. But he is not dead. And I cannot believe with some that he has stopped loving us. No. But how we loved our golden calf. He would not tolerate that. He is here. He is all about us. I do not know what he will do. But he is the God of all grace. It is impossible for him not to love, not to forgive.

My fingers are cramped. Why do I bother? I might as well write to a ghost. How do I know you are still alive? I am the madman of the desert. Maybe they will find this letter with my books, maybe it will be another boy looking for his goats, a thrown stone, a plinking against my gleaming skull. I ought to write something more for them. But what? That once there were half a million church buildings in Laodicea? That green ivy covered old stone chapels that had stood three hundred years? They will think I am telling a story. Remember how it was, my good Khartoum? We thought we would live a thousand years. A revival like Wesley's. The people of God would love us and our messages to them would shine like Orion.

Tom was the first of us to die. At least he died a martyr's death. A shotgun blast when he was trying to help those boys on drugs. Then Arthur died of cancer. But that kind of death was nothing compared to what came. Brother against brother. Family against family. Charismatic—I detest that term—against those who were not. You are a head Christian, we would sneer, but we are Spirit-filled Christians. Our movement is the movement of God. There is no other. How sublime our visions were. It is too bad mercy did not blind us. That would have changed everything. But who has room for mercy once they realize they alone have the truth? They must ram through all obstacles to get the truth out, especially if the obstacles are people. For the vision is always more important than the people, the idea always of greater import than the one lingering soul.

My good brother Khartoum. Once I thought the greatest failure was the failure of God's people. Church politics and gossip and viciousness and deception had become so much the norm, and God had worked with it for so many generations, we accepted it. Why rock the boat? God had tolerated the system this long, he would tolerate it forever. How congregations would bite and snap and growl at us, like Korah against Moses. Remember how we began to go down? Jeff to law school. Allen to pre-med. Hank to his taxi and then Wayne and his zookeeping. All the churches wanted was Phariseeism, all the congregations wanted was law, I was certain of it. If a pastor preached freedom or peace no one showed up. If he was dictatorial and dished out omnipotence, what they must do tomorrow, what they must eat or wear, when the world would end, what they must think, they flocked to him like skittish sheep. Wasn't it the same in Jesus' day? How many truly followed him? Did not most stay with the Law, with the Pharisees, and with the high priest? Our generation was no different. Tell us what to do. Freedom is too wide open and frightening. Grace is too uncertain. They wanted Egypt, my good Khartoum. They wanted Mount Sinai. Yes, it was slavery, but it was security, and freedom is not security. They did not put their souls in God's hands. They put their souls in the hands of those who said they were God's spokesmen the most loudly and the most cleverly. Let God be your security, a handful of us cried. Let his grace make you comfortable. Wrestle with him, like Jacob did, and know him. Follow the Cross. But no. They lusted for those who would organize their lives in a chaotic world and give them rules. Then they could be saved. I blamed them. I despised them. But it was we, we the shepherds, who failed them.

Perhaps, if you receive this, you will think, "Ah, the devil of the noonday sun has ahold of his mind and it is the devil's own ink that flows from his pen." No, my good brother, I write this by the light of a candle while God has showered stars upon me like a silver rain. I am shivering in my blanket but my mind is cool and clear, like a sweet oasis. I can see you growling out of your cabin on that island where the rain does not cease: "We did not fail God's people. They failed us." But who divided them into separate camps? Who turned them against each other? Who taught them how to fight? We. We split churches, encouraged the people to battle one another, to spit and to hiss and to scratch. We claimed it was all justified because we served a higher cause, like the seminary student who steals theology books he cannot afford because with these books God will help him preach a sermon on righteousness that will save many. It was not only the dictatorial and the autocratic leaders who wanted control. Every dreamer wanted his dream. We were so spiritual we only saw the God we imagined and we never imagined there could be another. We said we did it all for the love of God. But did we love God, my brother Khartoum? Or did we love our ideas and our theologies about God? Did we want to bring the people to Christ? Or did we want to bring the people to church, to fill our pews, to help us feel holy and successful and to ensure our salary packages? We competed for souls. Our soap was better than another church's soap. We slandered. We schemed. We enticed. So we shattered the great Church herself into a billion pieces. And we were astonished that having mutilated the Church for so many years, and in so many ways, and for so many holy reasons, that one morning all the king's horses and all the king's men could not put the Body together again. Our own congregations that had formed from splits continued to split apart before our eyes. Nothing we preached stopped this. There was always someone holier preaching something better. We had taught the people to run to this when we had taught them to run to us for the same reasons.

But even then we would not repent. We claimed that God approved of the shattering, that he actually saw unity where we saw disunity, and so we justified ourselves and the fresh divisions we caused, the new churches splitting from the old, the new denominations rising up in competition with all the others to proclaim the same God. The old wine was always bad, we had to break the bottles and get new ones, we had to. And when the Church in America collapsed we blamed the people, didn't we, Khartoum? We blamed the armies we'd created, not the generals. How could we blame the generals, how could we blame ourselves? All along we had been right. We were infallible. It was not our fault if people sinned. But surely God can take the pieces of the shattered Church and make a glorious stained glass image, we thought. Surely he can create an even more glorious Church with a mosaic. Surely the fragmentation is his will. Surely the breaking will make the Church more vulnerable and more accessible to this generation.

But here I am trembling in my cave, my good brother, and there you are in Laodicea, certain you will not have to become part of the diaspora, certain the Church will be resurrected to a greater glory. Perhaps one day. Perhaps tomorrow. Perhaps in another year. How long was it before the Jews kissed the stones of Jerusalem again?

My candle is guttering. I cannot write much more. Join me here if you decide to journey. We will pray. That is the good thing. To be Mary. We were the generation of Martha. Now, let us at least die at the Lord's feet, listening. My good Khartoum, for all I know this is Elijah's cave. Perhaps our Lord will tell me about the 7000 others. Perhaps he will tell me whom he will anoint after me. Perhaps he will assure me that nothing, after all, is lost, and that the war goes on until the last battle is won for the souls of the earth. Perhaps I will have one more mission before I enter his glory, something that will show me the glittering thread, something that Simeon saw, that Anna saw.

It is dark. When the sun rises I have my Greek and my Hebrew, the very words of God. There will be water and bread and warmth. Perhaps the wind of an angel's wings. The vista is enormous, as vast and as pure as our God, as endless as our prayers. Nothing more is needed. Was this not the way of the early Church? How can it be wrong to begin again in the same way?

The candle is almost gone. This page is the flashing of light and the breaking of shadows. My good brother, with all my heart, I love you. Christ be with you. I am sorry our generation was the Cross and not the Resurrection or the Parousia, as so many hoped. But without the Cross, how could any of us have entered life? In all our foolishness and pride, perhaps we have made more of a difference than we can possibly realize just now, with our spirits like broken jars. Perhaps we were the necessary death. What else could it mean when St. Paul wrote that the Church must fill up in herself the sufferings of Christ that remain? Clutch at this, my good Khartoum. It may be true. It may be the very essence of who we are. We became a faith founded on forgiveness that offered none. Now that we have no strength of our own, it remains to be seen what a God who knows what it is to forgive will be free to do in the world.

It is all starlight. My brother, until the day breaks and the morning star rises in our hearts, it is I, in this pottery of glory.

25

The Tiger Heart that
Pants Beneath

I had managed to elude the "nature red in tooth and claw" scenario for about ten years. I don't know how. Maybe the way I put the course on suffering together. Maybe the upbeat mood of most of the students made a difference. And the game of Pinzatski helped—this lichen-spattered boulder is the faithfulness of God, this pine cone is God seeding righteousness throughout the dark spaces of the earth, these fogs and mists represent the obscuring yet revealing shekinah glory of God. A friend named Arthur had developed the game along with his wife Ellen, years before cancer had claimed his life. It was based on a passage in Romans where St. Paul argues that God's divine nature—in fact, the very essence of who he is—can be seen clearly in what he has made. Looking back, I cannot say why we might conjecture that a volcano was the holiness of God but never move on and ask ourselves what the victims of a fatal eruption had to say about who he was. Perhaps it was a period of grace. If it was, it ended during the summer session at Duke.

It was my course on theodicy. As I had done every summer school since the late eighties, I encouraged the class to sign up for a canoe trip at the end of August. During this trip we would debate and discuss and we would play Pinzatski. All of Duke knew about Pinzatski by then. It was notorious. But it had helped resolve something of the nature of

God to many students to such an extent that it had become an indispensable teaching tool. Like air, it had to be there. So I made my invitation to the canoe trip one afternoon, placed the sign-up sheet on a table at the front of the classroom, and dismissed the students.

"My father was killed by a grizzly bear. He was fly-fishing with a friend from church. The pocket Bible he had in one of the pockets of his fishing vest was ripped to shreds and soaked in his blood. My father loved God and he loved God's creation. What does all that say about the nature of God?"

The students ceased to mill and chat. I hesitated. I thought I was being set up, that this might be an early fraternity initiation rite. But the young man's face was flushed and contorted. I did not know what to say.

"God did not send the grizzly," I answered lamely.

"But isn't this Pinzatski game about God's personality being revealed in everything that he has made? How is his personality revealed in a grizzly attack on a human?"

I said nothing.

"What about that mother who was killed defending her son from a cougar? What does a vicious cougar say about God? What does Pompeii or Mount St. Helen's say? Or a twister? Or a hurricane? What does all the violence in creation say about the nature of God?"

"The Fall," I stumbled.

"But St. Paul said that God was revealed in all of nature and he was talking about nature first century A.D., nature after Eden. I hear you always talking about the up side of nature, Professor. But nature kills without mercy. Does this mean that the God of love we read about in the scriptures is really a heartless monster?"

I bent over my lecture notes, shuffling them together, dropping my eyes.

"Mister...?" I said.

"Abraham Wilder."

"Mister Wilder. I hear you. This is obviously not the time for a detailed response. But I encourage you to sign up for the canoe trip. I promise you we will deal with this issue at a greater length then."

I walked over to him, extending my hand. He took it. I smiled but he did not. I was being given a reprieve. It would only be temporary. If I failed on the canoe trip, he would be finished with me and maybe with God too. For all I knew, so would others in the class. I returned to my office and buried myself in marking.

A summer session only lasts a couple of weeks. Soon I was up to my ears in preparations for the trip. But more critical than the lifejackets and paddles and freeze-dried food packages was the question: What aspect of God was in the marauding grizzly or the killer twister? I thought of one way out of it—toss the game of Pinzatski altogether. Perhaps the Romans text was unsound. Perhaps it was not included in earlier, more reliable manuscripts. I, the OT scholar, approached my NT colleagues only to be told—one was smirking, I thought—that the text was rock solid. Interpretation was another matter. But then, that was up to the individual, wasn't it? And, as my Roman Catholic and Orthodox friends pointed out, the teaching tradition of the Church.

If St. Paul had been talking about creation before the Fall my task would have been simple. I could then have argued that any image of God in nature was now flawed and not fully indicative of his true nature which could be seen most clearly in Christ and in Scripture. But no. St. Paul meant his first century Mediterranean sky, his first century mountains and meadows and deserts and, presumably, all the birds that flew, all the fish that swam, all the beasts that either hunted or were bleating prey. Had he been writing off the top of his head or had he thought his theology through? Romans was the cogently argued book, the one that law schools had used in the past to demonstrate the logical development of a train of thought. And there was the problem of the Holy Spirit—did I believe the text was inspired or was it just St. Paul having his day in court? I had seen scripture alter too many lives to the good. This was not the Epic of Gilgamesh. This was the Great Morality Play. It changed the human heart. So what then? Argue that the grizzly showed us Yahweh the Warrior, the God of Moses and Joshua, the God of the Exodus and the Conquest? That the savage death of his father who trusted in a merciful God was simply a symbolic representation of those who face the fury of God's wrath? That in his gory death he became a useful instrument for God's instruction? That the twisters and the volcanoes and the earthquakes showed us God's judgment? And that the victims showed us Hell?

It became more than answering Abraham Wilder around a crackling campfire. I needed to answer my own questions. Arthur Pinzatski had indicated that the cancer that was killing him had something to do

with the resurrection of the body and God coming to us in Christ—
"The Incarnation, my friend, the Incarnation. God's committed himself." Maybe I had deliberately suppressed my own most difficult questions about suffering in light of the positive aspects of Arthur's game.
Out of sight was out of mind. If no one close to you was suffering, you
didn't think about suffering, you didn't want to think about suffering,
why acknowledge its reality, it would lurch its way toward you soon
enough. Now there was Abraham Wilder's father dying with the grizzly
claws in his heart and the hot, stinking breath in his face. An end to a
life of faith? The signature of a loving, heavenly Father, rich in mercy
and grace?

Too soon the seven canoes were in the water and I stood by the
red one, Parousia, and Abraham was with me. He was staring down at
the swirling blue around his legs.

"It's a beautiful day, Abraham," I said. "And you'll find it's a beautiful river."

"Do you know what Melville said once about the Pacific?" Abraham
asked me. "On a calm, sunny day when it sparkled like this? He said
that there was a tiger heart that panted beneath the surface."

So our journey began. For seven days we would paddle and camp
and then the buses chartered by the university would take us back to
the man made. Until then, we were at the mercy of the God the game of
Pinzatski purportedly revealed.

The fire burned late the first night. We had only come ten miles.
There were a few aches and blisters but everyone was still full of energy
and excitement. Abraham said nothing while the others laughed and
chattered. His eyes rested solidly on me.

"What does night say about God?" I asked them. "That he dwells
in unapproachable light? Light that is like darkness to us because its
blazing purity blinds us? The night does not speak evil of God, does it?
If my skin colour were black, I would not appreciate it if everyone
associated its colour and my race with evil and, coincidentally, the white
race with purity. Darkness can be frightening to us, no matter what our
race, because it obscures. Who knows what is hiding in the darkness?
An armed robber? A dangerous animal? A ghost? But night itself is not
meant to be wicked. All the world falls in love with a starry night.
Doesn't it feel good to follow the sparks up? It seems they fasten themselves to the Pleiades. There is much we could not do well unless there

was night—rest, for one thing. Try taking on a night shift and sleeping during the day and you'll soon learn how blessed it is to rest in the darkness. How could we see the brilliance of the Milky Way without the night? Or the glory of a sunrise or sunset without the contrast? We could never spot a shooting star or watch the northern lights leap. St. Augustine would tell us that without the Fall we could never have seen the blaze of God's love exhibited in Christ's sacrifical death—how great a fall that merited so great a salvation. We would never know God's grace, bright streaks against our night. He would tell us that God chose to bring good out of evil rather than to disallow evil's very existence.

"So what can I say about Abraham's father? Or those killed by typhoons or tidal waves? Or those who eat poisonous mushrooms or who are bitten by rattlesnakes? Should there be no bears or plants or reptiles or winds or waters on this earth? A grizzly is equipped to defend itself and to hunt just as we have the ability to create tools or weapons to cultivate land or protect our families. Man can destroy man—what does that say about God? Didn't God make man in his own image? What do humans reveal about the nature of God? His love? His trust? His hope? What does creation reveal about its Creator when that creation becomes flawed? Are we only left with contrasts? Are we only left with Job and Ecclesiastes? Are we only left with Gethsemane and the Cross?"

Their young faces came and went in the fire. I stared at the golden coals. I had nothing more to say. I could not think. I could not resolve the matter.

"You're struggling, Professor," Abraham said, standing up. "But that's okay. I'd rather see you sweat than have you serve up some slick answer on a teflon pan. Good night."

The next day was thirty miles. The sun shone, the river helped us, there were no portages. We ate heartily. And then the fire was burning again.

A few had turned in early. Most squatted around the flames, exuding the mingled scent of various sweet sunscreens. We had played Pinzatski as we paddled that afternoon, just for an hour, calling back and forth between the canoes. Abraham had not joined in.

"It is still what it is," he told us at the fire. "My mother is a widow and my father was torn to pieces by one of God's creatures. The God he adored."

I shook my head, like the puzzle master scattering the pieces and hoping for a solution that will manifest itself in the new pattern. Images would not form in my head. So I continued to ask my own questions, voice my own struggles.

"What does a fallen world say about the living God? Today we looked at the river and at the sun and at the forests. It was good. But what about the deaths in the forest? A drowning in another part of the river? What does this say about the river? What does this say about the forest? That all is not as it appears on a sunny day? That there is always more below the surface? More behind the screen? Tell me—is this more about evil? Or is it about sin and redemption? Is the tragic about the triumph of evil? Or the possibility of good? Is Abraham's father's killing only about violent death that makes no sense? Or are we in the Garden of Gethsemane? Are the nails going in hard on Golgotha? Tell me—can there be love without struggle? Hope without suffering? Salvation without failure? Is God in the grizzly? Is God in Abraham's father? Is God in the dying of the man? What else can the Incarnation mean except that God bleeds? What else can the death of Abraham's father mean except that God suffers and dies? And perhaps there is more than that. Is your father dead, Abraham? Or does Golgotha say your father cannot die?"

Abraham's face was in the yellow and blue flames: "Heaven, Professor? Is that what death in the jaws of a grizzly means? It is well disguised. You would almost have to have a gnostic experience to see it. Is that what we all need on this canoe trip, Professor? A dose of gnosticism so that we can know the deep secrets of God?"

"No. Faith, perhaps."

"Then the grizzly is a test? Like Abraham and Isaac?"

"I do not say that. But if your father's death means God dies then perhaps the tiger heart that pants beneath is not always an evil or a destructive force. Maybe there is a more significant tiger than the tiger of violent death. Maybe there is one that can destroy the destroyer, a tiger that can kill the tiger, and in doing so set life at liberty to live forever. Who can reverse death and create life? Maybe the Creator is the tiger."

"No."

"Whose heart can beat even in death but the tiger who brings life out of death, good out of evil, restoration out of destruction?"

"Layer after layer after layer, Professor? Like peeling the onion?

Where is the heart? Where is the tiger heart?"

"Tell us who the tiger is, Abraham, and we will know where the heart is."

"No. He is dead. Horribly dead. And I will not let you or anyone else make his death beautiful or meaningful. I will not let you excuse God. I will not dishonour my father's tragedy by saying it is one of the hidden wonders of God, a perfect window on the mystery of redemption and resurrection. He is dead. He is dead."

It poured on us the next two days. Spirits plummeted. Hands and arms and backs burned with fatigue. Flesh was chilled. Clothes were soaked. We could not start any fires. We hunched under our canoes and ate cold food. We scarcely spoke. No one wanted to play Pinzatski. We crawled into our tents and tried to sleep. I dreamed of bears.

The fifth day was cool and bright. One of the students read us the psalm about the panting deer. We pushed the canoes out into the water. Abraham paddled grimly at my back. We did not talk. In all the canoes the only thing that united us was the rhythm of the paddling. There were four of us in each canoe. It was not the jerky, uncertain rhythm of the first two days. Skin and muscles were hardening. The paddling was strong and sure and it was beautiful. It was the only thing that gave me peace.

"Tomorrow is white water," I told them at our first fire in three days. "All of you have experience at this but remember that lifejackets remain mandatory, no matter how skilled you think you are. John's canoe will go first. I'll bring up the rear. If you get into trouble, go with the current and get to shore."

Everyone turned in. I poked at the fire with a stick. As the sparks whirled up around me, Abraham re-emerged from his tent and stood by the coals and flames, hands in his pockets, gazing into the leaping of the light.

"How can my father's death be a redemption?" he asked.

I shook my head and poked at another log. Fresh fire surged up.

"I try to think about what he would say if he could come back like the ghost of Hamlet's father. Would he be angry? Would he want to place any sort of blame? Would he lust for revenge against all the beasts of the earth? No. He would talk about creation groaning. Every tree and rock and animal suffering because of our sin. He often spoke about this when we fished together. He loved what God had made and he took it seriously that the wickedness of humanity had imposed a massive burden on all that he loved, animate or inanimate. The wolf took the fawn because of us. A cougar took a child. A volcano, doing what volcanoes do in a marred world, killed people. But he wanted the fairy tale: the wolf lies down with the lamb, the lion with the calf, a child can no longer be harmed by a poisonous snake, a cow and a bear graze side-by-side. He wanted the restoration of all things, he wanted the restoration of the earth and the sky and all creatures great and small, all forests, all meadows, all the seven seas. It seems fantastic to me, Biblical rhetoric and hyperbole. But he took it to heart. These end time demagogues talk about the rapture and the Antichrist and warfare and bloodshed. Dad's end time scenario was love and redemption. Man and woman would become what they were meant to be, maybe more. Yes, more. The suffering would result in a greater paradise than Eden, a greater humanity than Adam and Eve's. The redemption and the restoration would result in a greater creation. What would Dad say at this campfire? That he saw God in all of nature just as it stands right now. He'd see the promise of the morning in all the dark things that happened. He'd point out mercy and goodness and strength. He probably would say that his death was God's death and that therefore it carried with it the promise of resurrection, since the Incarnate God rose from the dead. The only heart beating beneath the skin of life and death and nature and tragedy would be divine. He'd tell me to look into this mass of fire and he'd whisper the tetragrammaton: Yahweh. Yahweh. I am that I am. I. Am."

He turned and knelt and disappeared into his tent. I put more wood on the fire, more than I should have. But I knew that I would not be able to sleep yet. Perhaps I would sleep by the fire. I sat and let the smoke find me for a moment. Then it cleared and I returned, my face bright and shining.

The river down from that camp was higher than I had counted on and faster. The heavy rains had changed everything. The rapids roared like a predator. We heard them grow and grow in strength as we approached, paddling. We rounded a bend and John's canoe was in, black on white on white. Four miles of it. John was steady and sure, gliding smoothly into the Vs where the water poured between the rocks. The rest of us followed as if we were all tied together. Strokes were smooth, bows pointing where they needed to point. Spray and light and flicks of sunshine like glass shattering all around us. Thank God, I thought. And then the fourth canoe slewed sideways and capsized and instantly numbers five and six piled into it and flipped over. Heads swooped down the rapids. I counted. Oh my God, my God, please.

"There are two missing!" shouted Abraham.

"Go right! Go right!" I screamed.

Our bow swung past the overturned canoes. Abraham leaped and disappeared. I paddled furiously.

"Beach it!" I yelled.

We yanked the canoe onto the gravel. I counted heads again. Three of the students were being helped further downstream by the other canoes. The rest of the swimmers were already ashore. But I could not see Abraham or the two that were missing. It was all white light. Then Abraham emerged on the other side of the river, swimming with another. The student sat bewildered where Abraham left him. I saw the other clinging to a rock. Abraham brought her to the shore. Then he was gone. He had slipped back into the water.

"Abraham!" I shouted. "Abraham! Get out of the river!"

His body popped up a moment later, much farther downstream, slack, knocked back and forth by the waves. John's canoe fished the body out. They paddled to shore and stretched Abraham across a spit of sand. I could see they were trying to resuscitate him. I sprang down the shoreline, over boulders and through pools, until I was with them. John was pushing on Abraham's chest. Someone was crying. "Come on, come on," another was pleading. I knelt. I felt for his pulse. We had lost him. But John would not stop.

"Enough," I said quietly.

John glared at me in a fury: "I am not a fatalist!" He bent over Abraham again while another student breathed at the correct intervals into Abraham's mouth. We waited. We prayed. The water was as bright as fire, the sky a blue sea. I heard a red-winged blackbird. The last canoe was beaching. The two Abraham had saved still sat on the opposite shore. We would have to get a canoe over to them. Four of the students had dragged the capsized canoes over the rocks and onto a gravel bar near us. A blue heron glided over our heads, swimming in the blue air.

John was crying, rocking back on his knees, his arms stiff. I took his place. I pushed. If the heart would beat. Fine spray showered us.

Finally I stopped, my arms aching and trembling. A student took my place. I sat on a rock. The canoes that had overturned did not look badly damaged. The two students on the other side of the river had made their way to a point just downstream of us where the water was flat. After another five minutes the students working on Abraham stopped and sat back in the gravel and the tufts of yellow grass. John began to recite the Lord's Prayer. We joined with him. Abraham lay, his curly black hair moving and moving in the wind. Then his fingers curled.

Tears cut through the grime on our faces. He coughed and stirred and sat up and still none of us went to him or spoke to him. It was a dream that was dreaming his resurrection.

"What is it?" he asked, looking at the crowd of us sitting about him and staring at him and crying.

I always planned that the campfire on the sixth night would be special, a celebration. I broke out the MARS bars. This was the greatest celebration I had ever seen. But it was as soundless as the far off stars. The fire flared and cracked, a few bar wrappers rustled, but we sat silently in a circle with our shoulders touching, several with their arms around one another. Abraham was wrapped in a thick blanket. The two he had saved sat close. A few hummed hymns and choruses and now and then the rest of us joined in, but no words were sung or spoken. The fire moved over all of us and once a star fell. I thought of Arthur Pinzatski and of Abraham's father. I slept. I woke lying by the fire with a blanket tucked around me. No one else was there. The fire was dying. A sudden desperate flaring revealed Abraham. I sat up. I could not see his face, only the shape of his darkness as he turned toward me.

"So, Professor. Will you call me Lazarus from now on behind my back?"

"I might."

"The water speaks of God. The fire speaks of God. Death speaks of God. How does that strike you?"

The fire ended. I could see nothing but a small red glow. Abraham stretched dark fingers over it.

"I guess everything says something. I don't have the language down. Do you?"

"No."

"Is creation groaning?"

"I'm sure of it."

"I ought to see a crucifixion in every tragedy then. That's our hope, isn't it? He is flesh as well as spirit and he walks us out of this. If he has no body, I only have another abstract philosophy. And the earth and its swans and lions have no words for us and no images. I might as well go back to the river and let it cover me. I don't need another philosophy. I need a face."

Now there was only a breath of smoke and the old burning stars.

"We can play Pinzatski on our last leg tomorrow, Professor?"

"I suppose we could."

"Fine. I am going to challenge you."

At breakfast we were grateful and then we slipped our canoes into the sweet water beyond the rapids. There was a breeze and a crinkled blue to paddle through. We did some singing and then the game of Pinzatski began, everyone playing everyone else at once. I had no opportunity to challenge my students. Abraham kept firing words at me and I had to keep rising to his cries: "Professor, those grey stumps, fourteen of them, isn't it? Professor, is that an osprey diving into that pool? Look. He has caught his fish. Well? Professor, that cloud has moved over the sun. What about that? See how the river bends here, Professor. What can this mean? What does this all say? And tell me about that great blue heron."

Laughter and shouting grew with the sun's strength and we carried on down our path, burning, blazing, riding the light, in no hurry, heaven and earth telling us its story, we struggling to understand, and God turning us round and round and round throughout Leo and Orion and the Pleiades and the Great Bear, telling us his name.

Afterword

These stories had their beginning in 1988 with the publication of "The Divine Game of Pinzatski." I suppose this story is the one best known. I wrote it for Loren and Mary Ruth Wilkinson in 1987, just after receiving my ThM degree from Regent College and just prior to moving from Vancouver. I left them a copy and didn't think much more about it until about a year later when Loren called me at my home in Winnipeg and insisted it must be published in *Crux*. The late Klaus Bockmuehl, who had graded my ThM thesis in 1987 while I waited with knocking knees, was editor of *Crux* at the time and was very encouraging and supportive of the story's publication. So I have Loren Wilkinson and Klaus Bockmuehl to thank for initiating what has developed into a ten-year relationship of storytelling and publishing.

It was really Don Lewis, however, who pushed me to keep on writing stories for *Crux*. He became editor of the quarterly shortly after Klaus Bockmuehl and I am certain that without Don's encouragement and persistence many of these stories would never have been published, let alone written. I am not sure how many theological journals publish poetry and stories on a regular basis. I don't think too many. I am grateful to Don and to those who have worked with him on *Crux* down through the years for creating a space for me to craft theology as story. I am also grateful to Luci Shaw who encouraged *Crux* to develop a permanent feature entitled "I Will Open My Mouth In Parables" that she felt I would have no problem supplying fresh material for. Thanks

211

to this, I have been called upon to write four stories a year for *Crux*, and there is nothing like a deadline to make a writer actually put his imagination on paper with some consistency. I doubt I would have enough to fill this volume except for those deadlines.

This collection came to the light of day thanks to Loren Wilkinson who brought Bill Reimer and myself together. I am grateful for the work Bill Reimer and Rob Clements have put into this project. It's wonderful to see all the stories together under one roof. They have been arranged basically in the order in which they were written and published. The exception would be the new stories that were written specifically for this collection and which, at least at the point of writing, have not been published anywhere else. These would include: "Good God"; "Wick"; "The Prophet of Kitsilano"; "White Man's God"; "Commodities"; "The Emperor of Ice Cream"; "The Legends of the Green Chapels"; and "The Tiger Heart That Pants Beneath."

I probably should be thanking many other people who have been dutifully labouring for *Crux* over the past decade and may have had much to do with the stories winding up neatly printed and grammatically correct in each issue. I suspect Dal Schindell and J. I. Packer have had a lot to do in this regard. Thank you, gentlemen. There are others whom I may not know and cannot name—I thank you also. If I am a better writer than I was ten years ago, it is due in part to the discipline of writing these stories. And their publication has opened up a new world to me.

Eugene Peterson is a man I have never met. Many times students or professors at Regent have asked me: "Have you met Eugene Peterson? Some of your stories sound like things he has said or that he might say." I have read a number of Eugene's books, his articles in *Crux*, and I have delighted in his earthy translation of Scripture in *The Message*. I have had the pleasure of speaking with him on the phone. I think I know a kindred spirit when I read one and hear one. He is presently about three hours drive due south of me in Lakeside, Montana and I am hopeful that one day I will be driving down to meet him and his wife. I am grateful to Eugene for agreeing to write the preface to this volume and in so doing to graciously endorse the writings of a man he has read but never known.

Each story is something of a child to its creator, with its own personality and history. The reader may detect changes in writing style and artistic expression if the stories are read from front to back. I have made a few small adjustments in some of the earlier stories but they appear here substantially as they were when first published, precisely because each of them honestly does have its own personality and its own way of telling a story. I have just let them be.

It remains to briefly mention the dedications that went with the original publication of several of the stories (as well as mention a few new ones). God bless you all for your love and your friendship: "The Divine Game of Pinzatski" and its sequel, "The Tiger Heart That Pants Beneath," are for Loren and Mary Ruth Wilkinson; "Lorine Jennifer Dies" is for Jennifer Doede; "The Professor's Theophany" is for Bob Doede; "The Body God" is for Gerry Fuller; "Boj" is for Mike Mason; "Our Saviour's Picture Not Made With Hands" is for Trevor Hart; "Mister Good Morning" is for Goldie Levy; "The Woodcutter" is for Richard Levy; "Good God" is for Paula Dunning; "The Legends of the Green Chapels" is for Stephen Dunning; "White Man's God" is for Andy Russell; "The Prophet of Kitsilano" is for Bob Hanson; "The Emperor of Ice Cream" is for Pastor Gary Wilkerson and The Peak Community Church of Denver, Colorado.

October 1, 1998   —Murray Andrew Pura
Waterton-Glacier International Peace Park

> *all jesus did that day was tell stories—a long*
> *storytelling afternoon*
> *his storytelling fulfilled the prophecy*
> *i will open my mouth and tell stories*
> *i will bring out into the open things hidden*
> *since the world's first day*

matthew 13.35

www.ingramcontent.com/pod-product-compliance
Lightning Source LLC
Chambersburg PA
CBHW031249090426

42742CB00007B/382